HANDS ACROSS MICHIGAN

Tradition Bearers

HANDS ACROSS MICHIGAN

Tradition Bearers

BY ALAN R. KAMUDA

Detroit Free Press

In cooperation with Michigan State University Museum
and the Historical Society of Michigan

The Historical Society
of Michigan

Established in 1828

HANDS ACROSS MICHIGAN
Tradition Bearers

Author: Alan R. Kamuda
Editor: Nancy E. Dunn
Design: Lee Yarosh
Copy editors: Nancy E. Dunn, Patricia Foley
Graphic artist: Martha Thierry
Jacket photo of author by Tony Spina
Hands Across Michigan logo by James Denk
Color and black-and-white printing
by Diane A. Bond

Published by the Detroit Free Press
Detroit, Michigan 48226

MANUFACTURED IN THE UNITED STATES OF AMERICA

ISBN 0-937247-55-3

"A People That Take No Pride in the Noble Achievements of Remote Ancestors Will Never Achieve Anything Worthy to be Remembered with Pride by Remote Generations."

– Macaulay

Table of contents

Po-Ling Cheng is an 84-year-old Chinese calligrapher. A recent immigrant to the United States, he brought with him a distinctive art that arose from the earliest form of writing. Cheng combines poetry, prose and philosophy with his skill and teaches those with the will to learn. Page 120.

Foreword

Oh, the stories they could tell …

I had just spent the day with Harriet and Charles Shedawin. They showed me how they made baskets from trees and they told me what it was like growing up as American Indians in the 20th Century.

As I left their home at the Soo and headed toward Marquette, their story took over my mind. It was late in the afternoon on a gray day in early spring 1987, and mine was the only car on M-28.

Instead of traveling forward in time, my mind was traveling backward. Back to the early days of this century when Harriet was growing up on Sugar Island. I walked with her as she went door-to-door peddling her baskets, beautiful black ash baskets she had worked weeks on, hoping to earn a nickel, maybe a dime, happy to trade one for a peanut butter sandwich or an old pair of shoes.

I wanted to learn more.

Harriet's story awakened me to the history of this place we call Michigan. I wanted to learn who had moved here and why.

The next stop was Negaunee to see Tynie Rivers. The voyage continued, and it is still going on. My teachers have been Russell Johnson in Strongs, Donna Esch in Fairview, Isaiah (Doctor) Ross in Flint, Sonnie Perez in Livonia — and so many more.

In all the stories in "Hands Across Michigan: Tradition Bearers," I describe the ethnic heritage of the artists using the terms they prefer in referring to themselves. In some of the stories I might use the name "Chippewa," in others "Ojibwa," in others *Anishnabe* (ah-neesh-NAH-beh) — all words used to describe the same tribe. I use the terms they use because the stories are theirs, not mine.

Alan R. Kamuda

Three Amish girls enter their one-room schoolhouse north of Mio. The Amish maintain a lifestyle that hasn't changed much in the almost 100 years they have been calling Michigan home. Page 60.

Preface

It's no wonder that Michigan's most noticeable feature is that it looks like a giant hand. Michigan holds all the people of the world.

Surrounded by the world's greatest lakes, blessed with natural resources beyond even the wildest dreams, and home to the mightiest industrial explosion ever, Michigan's two peninsulas have attracted people from around the globe. Loggers from Canada, sailors from the Atlantic Coasts, miners from Cornwall, farmers from Germany, teachers from New England, and factory workers from the South have joined Michigan's native people to form a human mosaic of the whole world. Even now, years after the virgin lumber has been taken, the good copper mined and much of the car business moved, Michigan attracts people from around the globe. They come to work with their hands, use their heads and follow their hearts. People do not leave the old ways behind them; they bring the old ways with them.

The way people cook, play, work; the way they teach, entertain themselves, celebrate and grieve — all are the traditions of their people. These folkways have been handed down from mothers and fathers to sons and daughters, from generation to generation, from all parts of the world, to Michigan.

Detroit Free Press Staff Photographer Alan R. Kamuda has been pursuing these traditions for years. With a keen ear, a sharp eye and his camera, Kamuda has witnessed simple stories that echo with the profound reverberations of trackless history and far-off lands. The people in this volume are as new to Michigan as this morning, but as old as the Great Lakes; as near as the other side of the street, but as exotic as the other side of the Earth.

In "Hands Across Michigan: Tradition Bearers," Kamuda introduces you to people as he has come to know them: one at a time, honestly, doing simple things that speak of their families, their people, their lives. Meet fiddle players, carvers, weavers and fishers; painters, singers, dancers and cooks. As you page through "Hands Across Michigan," you will be surprised at how much more you can learn with your eyes than with your ears. The ways in which these people will meet you, teach you, reach you, know no linguistic or nationalistic boundaries. In fact, you may be surprised to see how close some of these traditions are to the ways of your own people.

NEAL SHINE, publisher
Detroit Free Press

Les Raber, on the left, and Art Moilanen get together for a jam session at the music jamboree held every year in Aura, a small Upper Peninsula town in the middle of the Point Abbaye Peninsula, north of L'Anse. Raber's story is on page 70 and Moilanen's on page 30.

Introduction

C. Kurt Dewhurst

We are all tradition bearers. We all draw upon traditional knowledge, whether it be in preparing a favorite family recipe, celebrating a religious holiday such as Christmas or a rite of passage such as a bar mitzvah, making an ice fishing decoy or tying a fly for fishing.

Traditional folk culture is local in character. It changes little over time and often is ethnically or occupationally based. Participation in it encourages adherence to an order that arises from well-established community aesthetics. Stories, crafts, foodways and customs generally are passed on orally or by example from one person to another within a tradition that deeply values careful observation and a respect for communally retained knowledge.

While we are all tradition bearers — and while cultural allegiance and unity are the values that are dominant forces in traditional folk communities — each tradition has its masters across Michigan. Recognized in their communities and by fellow practitioners, these masters not only have learned the techniques and craftsmanship required to excel but also have a deeper and richer understanding of the history, character and meanings associated with their traditions.

For the tradition bearers in this book, the development of their artistic expression and cultural knowledge — as well as the sharing of that knowledge with others — is central to their lives.

Tradition Bearers

The image of the hand has special meaning to the people of Michigan. Michiganders use their hands as portable maps of the Lower Peninsula and they use their three extended fingers to represent the Upper Peninsula, pointing out where they live, where they were born or where they have a favorite haunt. This book conveys another, though somewhat less tangible, image of the hands of diverse tradition bearers from throughout the state. Michigan has been recognized as one of the most culturally diverse states in the Union. More ethnic groups than in virtually every other state, the extremes associated with industrial and rural life, an endless variety of occupations — all these appear within two peninsulas separated by water. Despite this variety of life experience, a unifying element remains: the wealth of Michigan traditions expressed in the skilled hands of tradition bearers.

The making of things and the grasping of the knowledge involved in crafting and shaping traditional objects offer another instructive image. In his book, "Grasping Things," Simon J. Bronner writes: "Together, sight and touch provide the basis for grasping things, which is at the foundation of material life … Touch takes on importance because its association with hands implies the grip of possession. In conversation, 'wanting to see something' is weaker than 'wanting to get my hands on something' …" Objects made by human hands bring human design and personality outward.[1]

This book strives to bring the lessons and personalities of tradition bearers even farther outward.

Tradition Bearers Communicate Cultural Meanings

Some art historians believe that objects speak for themselves, that they convey a set of universally agreed-upon meanings or feelings. However, objects do not speak for themselves; they are always interpreted. Depending on whether they are interpreted by people within a group or those outside, the results often are dramatically different.

Glen VanAntwerp's cedar fan carving, shown on the front and back of the jacket of this book and described within the pages, provides a fine example. People who come from outside the tradition are galvanized by the complexity and subtlety of the technique of carving a cedar fan or a bird from one piece of wood. Those within the tradition know that this practice was introduced by Scandinavian immigrants who came to work in Michigan lumber camps. Initially viewed as merely a whittler's trick, the technique is used to carve birds that hang over holiday tables to represent the Christian symbol of the Holy Ghost, blending religious and family traditions with the lumberman's. Glen VanAntwerp, as a student and a master of his tradition, carries on the work of his great-great-grandfather, his great-grandfather, his grandfather and his father. Now Glen has passed it on to his son and daughter.

Within the family, these tradition bearers clearly communicate cultural meanings that extend beyond the mastery of carving a cedar fan. Through research at Michigan State University Museum, Glen VanAntwerp learned of the work of another cedar fan carver, John Smedley. While they were from different areas of Michigan, they were like brothers when they met, sharing their carving traditions and the meanings that were passed along to them. It is John Smedley's poem about cedar fan carving that appears, along with Glen's hands at work, on the jacket of this book. Two men, one tradition; they are as one.

Tradition Bearers Convey Enjoyment

Traditions *do* bring people together. Hands touch in the teaching of a tradition. People come together to learn, to practice, to do, to enjoy, with their traditions as the link. The sewing circle quilters of St. Mary's Church in Lake Leelanau have met regularly for years to share their quilting secrets — and simply to enjoy quilting with one another. They come together to make quilts to help the church's school, but they share family events, joys and sorrows as they explore the color and beauty of making quilts. While most quilt tops begin at the home of a single quilter, joining together to complete the work allows the group the pleasure that comes with communal creativity.

Tradition Bearers Express Feelings and Emotions

Traditions are never devoid of emotions. Donald Naganashe, who makes small boxes using porcupine quills and birch bark in the Ottawa and Chippewa manner, has said of his work, "I try to do what was passed on to me by my grandma. This is the only way I can enhance my feelings." Naganashe's sustenance of a centuries-old practice goes beyond a desire to continue the art forms of his ancestors. Naganashe expresses his strong, warm feelings for those who taught him. Each box helps him connect with those who went before him, and therefore the act of creation serves as an emotional message for both the maker and those who are associated with his mastery of this tradition.

Tradition Bearers Craft Identity

Dwight (Bucko) Teeple, a Chippewa Indian, set out on a journey to rediscover tribal ways. Teeple's vision quest after his service in the military and his ongoing personal quest to discover traditional beliefs have led him to conclude that "life is a learning that we must never stop." Our traditions are shaped by the past but must be sustained by practice and personal journeys.

Tradition Bearers Teach

The passing on of knowledge within a family, a community or neighborhood or some other group is folk tradition in action. Jay Stephan, an Au Sable River boat builder and guide, has accumulated knowledge through a lifetime of observing local tradition and joining in it. Over the years, river guides such as Stephan have been a primary force in the maintenance and transmission of river culture. Not only do these individuals build boats, they also share their knowledge of the history and nuances of fishing the Au Sable. When Stephan was asked how he learned the proportions of an Au Sable River boat, he remarked, referring to his teacher: "Bud had everything in his head just as I do."

Tradition Bearers Demonstrate the Variety and Complexity of Traditions

Often, there are certain factors, such as religious beliefs, that are an integral part of what tradition bearers do. Roy Yoder and his family make furniture; actually they make Amish furniture. Their religious doctrine provides a framework for how they make their hickory rockers and tables. Their religious convictions guide them in deciding when to work, what power sources are acceptable, how to obtain materials, how to market their furniture and how to divide the labor in their family — Roy and his wife, Mary, and their son, Merle, and daughter, Celesta. To understand, one must grasp what it means to be Amish — and what being Amish means to the Yoder family. Roy Yoder has developed a strong and complex connection to the natural world that makes his woodworking an extension of his Amish world view. He takes pride in making something that lasts, "… an heirloom, a passed-down thing that people use."

A Helping Hand

"Hands Across Michigan: Tradition Bearers" has been developed in partnership with the Detroit Free Press and the Historical Society of Michigan as part of Michigan State University Museum's commitment to the documentation and presentation of Michigan's traditional arts.

Our history as individuals and as a society manifests itself in our living traditions. They are our cultural resources for tomorrow. In recognizing the art that is so concretely manifested by the tradition bearers in this book, we are celebrating the power and persistence of all traditional culture in Michigan.

This book reminds us that while we all are tradition bearers, there are masters of old traditions and of emerging traditions among us. We have much to learn from them. We need to learn how to look for these people. When we find them, we must honor their mastery and knowledge. If we do, the generations will join hands. The apprentices of today will become the masters of tomorrow.

C. Kurt Dewhurst, PhD, is director of Michigan State University Museum and an associate professor in the Department of English at MSU.

[1] "Grasping Things: Folk Material Culture and Mass Society in America," by Simon J. Bronner. The University Press of Kentucky, 1986, p. 5.

The Michigan Traditional Arts Program
of Michigan State University Museum

The Michigan Traditional Arts Program of Michigan State University Museum serves as a state center for the traditional arts — folk traditions. The program provides consulting services and develops and maintains a collection of traditional arts and the Michigan Folklife Research Collections.

Major activities include:

◆ The annual Festival of Michigan Folklife on the MSU campus in East Lansing.

◆ The Michigan Heritage Awards, presented annually to master artists who continue the traditions of their families or communities with excellence and authenticity (See page 134 for a complete list of Michigan Heritage Award winners).

◆ The Michigan Traditional Arts Apprenticeship Program, a joint effort of the museum, the Michigan Council for the Arts and Cultural Affairs and the National Endowment for the Arts.

◆ The Michigan Quilt Project, begun in 1984 to locate, document and collect information and materials on Michigan quilts and quilters.

◆ The Folkpatterns Project, a joint effort of MSU museum and the 4-H youth programs of the Cooperative Extension Service, begun in 1979 with funds from the National Endowment for the Humanities to guide the young participants as they document folkways and historical identities of their families and communities.

◆ The Traditional Arts Traveling Exhibitions, through which some of the exhibitions of the Michigan Traditional Arts Program are made available for travel to other sites.

◆ The Michigan Traditional Arts Technical Services Program, which reaches out to offer help to community and individual efforts, especially those with meager resources.

◆ McDonald's/MSU Museum GospelFest, a major Detroit gospel choir competition and an educational, interpretive showcase of African-American music every year during the Freedom Festival.

◆ MSU American Indian Heritage Pow Wow featuring children's hands-on activities and, for all ages, lessons in the history and significance of the powwow as an activity that passes down traditions.

◆ Outreach services through which the Michigan Traditional Arts Program assists with research and education.

To learn more about the documentation and presentation of Michigan traditional arts, contact Michigan State University Museum in East Lansing at 517-355-2370.

Frank Ettawageshik re-creates the pottery of his Odawa Indian ancestors at his home in Karlin. He gathers natural materials and uses methods developed centuries ago in order to keep the Odawa ways from being forgotten. Page 46.

For Margaret and Stanley Kamuda

*Thank you for teaching me to watch other people
and to learn from what they do.*

Presque Isle River

Gogebic County

Upper Peninsula

Calumet ◆ ◆ Mohawk

Toivola ◆

Mass City ◆

Lake Superior

Ironwood ◆

Negaunee ◆

Whitefish Bay

Sault Ste. Marie ◆

Pendills Bay

Newberry ◆ ◆ ◆ Strongs

Hulbert Corners

Curtis ◆

DeTour Village ◆

0 Miles 30

Lake Michigan

Russell Johnson

lumberman's blacksmith

There are many stereotypes of north woodsmen, but 75-year-old Russell Johnson is an original.

Johnson, a lumberman's blacksmith, is the third generation to do the work that brought his grandfather from Sweden to Chippewa County.

Plaid shirts, suspenders and boots are his uniform. His gray hair is always covered with a broad-brimmed hat that Johnson began wearing long before Indiana Jones.

Johnson's hands, hands that can still swing an 8-pound hammer against an anvil the way his grandfather did, always need washing. Visitors to his work shed tiptoe through the clutter accumulated in the 50 years he's been working there.

Anyone approaching the small travel trailer that Johnson calls home might hear him yelling. One glance through the front door — it's always open when he's around — and it's obvious he's only reading to himself.

Johnson always talks loud and fast. Loud, so he can hear himself without putting a fresh battery in his hearing aid, and fast, to keep up with his mind, which zooms along like the logging trucks on Upper Peninsula roads.

Johnson makes axes to cut down trees and long, flat skidders to haul them. He can take a railroad spike, and after an hour in his work shed — heating the spike and pounding it so hard that sparks fly — he has a small hatchet. Loggers come to Russell's place to have him repair equipment that's getting harder to buy. Visitors stop by to see whether there are any tools lying around that they can bid on.

Johnson's work shed becomes a classroom when grandson Chad comes over. Russell is teaching Chad how to pound the anvil and make the tools the Johnsons have been hammering out for 100 years.

Three generations of Johnsons are shown with the tools of the profession practiced by two generations of Johnsons before them in the eastern Upper Peninsula — blacksmithing for the lumber trade. From left is Chad, 17, Russell Johnson's grandson; Russell's son, Rudy, 42; and the man who has taught them both, 75-year-old Russell Johnson. Like the anvil in the foreground, the work requires endurance and strength. Rudy makes his living in lumbering and real estate but works with his dad whenever he can, making tools and other things he needs. "When you're holding the iron, you learn a lot. It's surprising how much you pick up just by watching your father. You learn without knowing it."

Clockwise, from left: Russell Johnson outside his work shed in the summer of 1992. There is so much equipment on his 20 acres that it is hard to tell where his work area stops. He lives in a trailer at the front of the property. Inside the work shed, Johnson strikes a piece of metal he has just heated to flatten it. When the sparks stop flying and the metal cools, he will have a runner to be attached to the bottom of a wood-hauling sleigh to move big logs out of woodlots. Later, Johnson reads aloud to himself, unwinding at home with a good story to close out a long workday.

Clockwise, from left: Johnson shows off an evener he made in his forge. An evener is attached to the front of a freight-hauling dray or sleigh and then to the horses so they pull evenly. At right, grandfather and grandson bore a hole in a runner they are repairing. Chad, a senior at Brimley High School in Brimley, started working with his grandpa when he was a little boy. It's fun being around the forge, says Chad. "I learned from him that it ain't so hard to fix things once you know how to do it." Chad built his own forge a few years ago and found that he liked making hatchets and fire pokers and other things he could use. Below, Russell Johnson goes to the post office in Strongs to collect his mail and catch up on the news. The area where Johnson lives and works is about 30 miles west of Sault Ste. Marie just off M-28 in Chippewa County.

Russell Johnson has a small combo's worth of instruments in his trailer and grabs every one of them now and then to play a tune, sing a song and get away from it all for a while. Johnson can play "anything with strings," says his son, Rudy. Johnson has taught himself to play banjo, accordion, guitar, piano and organ. "If he hears a song twice, he can play it," Rudy says. Years ago, Russell Johnson played in bands and called square dances.

Jo Harrison

cabin keeper

"At first, they called this the 'Candy Place,' " said Josephine Harrison, for many years the owner, manager and gas station attendant of the Macjo Motel on M-28 in the eastern Upper Peninsula.

"My husband McKinley (McKinley + Josephine = Macjo) was real sick back in the '60s, and he felt sorry for me because every spring, after the snow melted, I had to scrape off and redo the varnish on all the cabins.

"Because the paint would hold up better than the varnish, he told me to paint them," said Harrison, 88.

"He said, 'Paint them different colors,' so I did. On each cabin I'd paint one board green, the next pink, the next brown, the next yellow.

"When he saw what I had done, he said, 'My God, what have you done? What I meant was to paint each cabin a different color.'

"But after a while he started saying, 'I like it. Let's leave it that way.' "

The Harrisons moved to the UP from Pontiac in 1945, when McKinley was told he was terminally ill with a lung ailment.

"He said if I only have two more breaths, I want to breathe the northern air," Josephine said. "It must have done some good. The three weeks they said he had left turned into 28 years."

After McKinley died in 1973, Josephine ran the Macjo but decided to sell in 1991. "If you're your own boss," she said, "you never have the day off.

"You don't get to see much when you get tied up with business," she said before the sale.

"That's what I intend to do when I retire, go out and see things. I want to live it up in my second childhood, run around and gab, gab, gab."

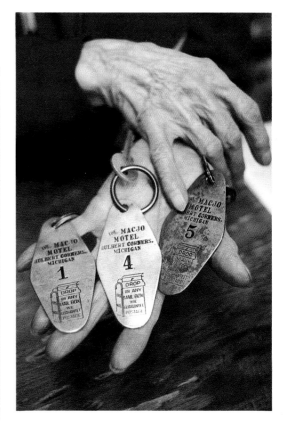

Merchandise ranging from motor oil to razor blades to cough drops is stacked on the shelves, hanging on pegs, or stashed in jars on the counter of Josephine Harrison's combination general store and gas station. The location — Hulbert Corners, at M-28 and Hulbert Road in Chippewa County — makes it a place where regular customers stop in to catch up on the news. M-28 is the east-west route across the middle of the Upper Peninsula, from just south of Sault Ste. Marie almost to Wisconsin. Harrison holds the keys to three of her six cabins at the Macjo — four one-room units and two units with two rooms each and enough space to sleep six people.

Macjo Motel owner and manager Josephine Harrison also is the gas station attendant. "I full-serve here, except for the snowmobilers. They always want to do it themselves," she says. The business has taught her a lot about car repairs and auto parts. At left, she helps Hulbert resident Jack Callender select the correct alternator belt for his 1984 Ford F250 pickup. In the photo above, the up-and-down stripes Josephine Harrison painted on the Macjo's cabins can be seen on the right. Below, the station's lamps shine like beacons to travelers along M-28 in early 1991.

Bucko Teeple

seeker of tradition

Dwight (Bucko) Teeple of Sault Ste. Marie is a storyteller, but the story he tells is a story he had to find.

"I was born in a cabin on Lake Superior and my great-grandma delivered me," said Teeple, 44.

"I was raised by my family to be proud of who I was as an Indian person. My grandma taught me to be proud of my heritage. But after I went into the military, I went on a vision quest.

"I spent four days and four nights on *Ile Parisienne* in Whitefish Bay. There was total abstinence. No food. No water. It was an inward journey for me. It made me more aware of who I was and what was around me. It made me more aware of nature."

Teeple, whose native name is *Wabun-Anung,* or Morning Star, started traveling around the country to discover more about his culture's traditional beliefs. "I've learned the equal importance of the environment around us, that life is a learning that we must never stop."

Teeple has taken his journey outward and shares it with fellow *Anishnabek* in the Sault Ste. Marie Tribe of Chippewa Indians and the Bay Mills Indian Community.

"A lot more people are looking to the traditional ways for their beliefs," said Teeple, who holds a bachelor of science degree in social studies, "and I am trying to help them."

"Whenever I'm asked to do something, I do it. Ceremonies for the seasons, naming ceremonies, funerals and prayers in sweat lodges. I'm trying to bring more awareness of the *Anishnabe* society to all humans.

"Part of my responsibility to the tribe is educating people that we have Indians who are progressive enough to compete in today's business market and still carry traditional beliefs."

After he left the U.S. military in the early 1970s, Bucko Teeple vowed to go "back to my roots, the traditional ways." To help fellow *Anishnabe* people learn about their heritage, he participates in prayer services, naming rituals, funerals and other rites. To dispel the Hollywood image of how Indians dressed, he wears traditional clothing for special occasions. On his head he wears a roach of porcupine and deer hair. Over his chest is a protective breastplate made of bones, brass and leather. The beadwork on his cuffs is a traditional *Anishnabe* floral pattern. In his left hand is a burled wood knot war club; his right hand holds a feather fan used to help build fires to heat stones for sweat lodge ceremonies. Sweat lodges are places of healing for body and spirit.

A bustle made of eagle feathers and beadwork is worn on the lower back as part of Bucko Teeple's ritual dress. This one has rows of beadwork and the initials AIM, for American Indian Movement. Teeple was once active in the organization but in recent years has concentrated on his work with the Sault Ste. Marie Tribe of Chippewa Indians and the Bay Mills Indian Community. Teeple holds a federal permit to possess eagle feathers.

Bucko Teeple builds a sweat lodge in spring 1992. He gathers small saplings from the forest, cuts and bends them gently, then ties them together to form the frame. For centuries, sweat lodges have been places of healing and renewal. The shape symbolizes the womb of Mother Earth because "the Earth is our real mother; she takes care of all our physical needs," says Teeple, who gathers stones from the Lake Superior shore to be heated and used in the lodge.

Lodges vary in size but share the same purpose: to foster mental, spiritual and physical renewal for the people who gather for prayer. The eagle feather fan is used to help create the fire which heats the rocks. The red-hot rocks are then brought inside the lodge and placed in a pit where water is poured over them to make steam for purification.

Harriet Shedawin

black ash basket maker

"We don't do it for the money," said Harriet Shedawin (SHED-ah-win). "People who do it for money lose the value."

Shedawin's attitude toward traditional Indian basket making changed over the years. When she was a child on Sugar Island, just east of Sault Ste. Marie, "I clothed myself by making baskets. We had to do this; it was our survival."

Shedawin, a Chippewa Indian, died in 1991 at age 73. She had vivid memories of her girlhood: "We used to come to town and peddle the baskets door-to-door, trade them for food, because we were so poor. I enjoyed selling them for 5 cents."

The baskets provided more than food as she grew up; she made them so she could buy alcohol. After sobering up and marrying her longtime friend Charles, Harriet took her basket making to powwows and local get-togethers. She used the ancient art to bring the youth close to her, so they would talk and she and Charles could help them fight the urge to drink.

The baskets went from providing food to providing drink, and then hope. What didn't change was the way they were made. Harriet and Charles started by finding strong specimens of black ash. They cut four-foot logs, removed the bark and notched the wood. They sliced off strips about an inch-and-a-half wide and thin enough to bend easily. After the strips were dry, Harriet Shedawin separated them with a drawknife and pulled them apart two or three times, getting them down to a workable thickness.

She didn't want to see her art die and would go to schools to demonstrate it whenever she was asked. "It taught me patience, tolerance, strength and value in myself," she said.

Harriet Shedawin shows off the only sample of her work she kept in the house, a small cone basket with a delicate pattern around the outside. She taught her art to others so it would live on. When she died in 1991, her obituary in the tribal newspaper, written by family friend Janice Hietikko, paid tribute to Harriet Shedawin's generosity and love of life: "Whoever sat by her side … will miss her … a *chi megwech* ('great thank you' in Ojibwa). Swinging Lady, we love you."

Making baskets requires a heavy hand and a delicate touch. Charles Shedawin pounds long pieces of wood from a log. Black ash is used because it is strong yet very flexible. Above are the strips he has removed after 15 minutes of pounding and pulling. Harriet uses her teeth to hold the strips as she pulls them apart into thinner pieces. "Everything is done by eye, nothing measured," she said. Charles Shedawin continues to make baskets the way Harriet taught him.

Harriet and Charles Shedawin stand in front of their house at Sault Ste. Marie in 1987. They met in 1953 and married in 1975 after they both conquered alcoholism. The Sault Ste. Marie Tribe of Chippewa named the reservation's substance abuse center after Harriet, thanking her for the work she did with the young people.

Tynie Rivers

rug weaver

It's hard to guess how many rugs have come out of the basement of Tynie Rivers' home in Negaunee, near Marquette. But, as Tynie said, "nearly every state in the union has at least one of my rugs in it."

Around 1932, she started using her mother's loom to make rugs from old drapes and bedspreads — "they make really nice rugs" — as well as overalls and other castoffs. Over the years she began working in more modern items such as garbage bags and bread wrappers. "Even my own clothes get used. When they get worn out, they go for rugs.

"I learned how to make rugs the hardest way," she said. "I learned by my own mistakes. But I really wouldn't have learned anything if I hadn't learned it from my mom."

When Rivers' mother died in 1947, her father built her a new loom using pieces from her mother's loom that were more than a hundred years old. For 41 years after that, Rivers used that weaving machine to create beautiful rugs from scraps. She made them to order from odds and ends provided by her customers. She sorted their rags, snipped off the seams and cut strips that could be threaded into her loom.

"Sometimes they send me a set of brand new drapes to make a rug," Tynie said in 1987. "I really hate cutting up good stuff like that, stuff that somebody could still use."

Her work turned into a love over the years. "I do it as a hobby, not to get rich. I hope to have more time to do more rugs, but I don't need any more rags. I don't think I'll ever finish the rags I already have."

Tynie Rivers died in 1988 at age 79. Her granddaughter Debra has since moved into her house and now makes rugs on the loom her great-grandfather built.

Tynie Rivers takes a break in her basement workshop in 1987. She enjoyed working there but sometimes found it too cold, despite the wood-burning stove. A box of rags sits nearby, ready to be woven into rugs. She would sort through them and pick colors that would create distinctive patterns when worked into a rug on her loom. Rug making is a tradition among Finnish Americans in the Upper Peninsula.

Clockwise, from bottom: Tynie Rivers prepares to add a strip of cloth to the rug she is making on her loom. Strips of fabric are worked crosswise into the long strands, called the warp, that are stretched out on the loom. The strands bind the strips tightly to make a rug. Rivers shows some of her finished work. She enjoyed making different-colored rug patterns using the rags she had on hand, playing bright colors against each other to make eye-catching designs.

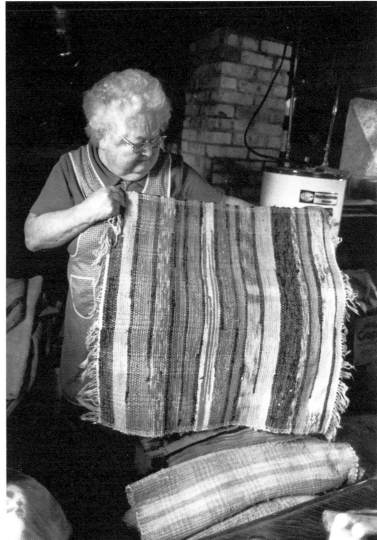

Ellen Angman

rug weaver

When Ellen Angman wanted her neighbor to make her a few rag rugs, she was turned down flat. Instead, the neighbor gave her something better — lessons, so she could make her own.

That was more than 50 years ago, but Angman remembers it as well as she remembers how to loom rags, string and odd pieces of cloth into beautiful floor coverings.

"I asked my neighbor, Mary Erkkila, to make a few rugs for me," recalled the 85-year-old great-grandmother, who has called the Keweenaw Peninsula home for more than 60 years.

"She just told me, 'No, make your own.' A loom to me was just a pile of string. I didn't know a thing about making rugs. But Mrs. Erkkila taught me everything. She taught me how to braid the warp, load the loom and weave the rugs. And when I had learned it all, she gave me the loom she was teaching me with so I could keep on making them."

Ellen Angman returned the favor by teaching others how to make rugs. She still uses the loom she received from Mary Erkkila.

"I first had it in the garage, then moved it to the granary, then the horse stalls. Now it sits in the old chicken coop." She and her husband, Edward, who died in 1964, relied on a dairy herd for income when their children were young. She made and sold her rugs to supplement their earnings.

Fifty years ago, the rugs — usually three feet wide — went for 35 cents a yard. Now, they sell for about $12 a yard.

"One doesn't get rich making rugs," said Angman. Today, she spends the long days of summer (and winter) making rugs as presents for her "42 or 43" great-grandkids.

"I don't do it for the money. I do it because I love the work."

Clockwise, from left: Balls of material sit near the loom in the old chicken coop on Ellen Angman's farm near Calumet. In years past, Angman made and sold rugs, but these days she looms them for her great-grandkids. Angman's neighbor and rug-making pupil Jean Johnson practices on the loom in the fall of 1992 while Angman prepares more fabric by removing seams and cutting or ripping the large pieces into long strips. She will then wind the strips into neat balls and toss them into the bin to be used to make rugs. Finished rugs — fringed and colorful — are shaken out and stacked up in a pile. Angman sometimes makes more than one rug of the same design; sometimes she lets her imagination run free. When it's time to collect the mail, Angman heads down the long driveway of the farm where she has lived since 1928. In the winter, she wears snowshoes for the trip. Cotton string, like the skein Angman is holding, will be put on the loom lengthwise to form the warp in the rug-weaving process.

Anna Lassila

rug maker

"My mother had a loom, but I never saw her use it," said Anna Lassila (LASS-ill-ah).

Lassila, who has spent the better part of her 83 years in the western Upper Peninsula, grew up on a farm near Mass City.

"My mom was always too busy to weave," said Lassila. "I learned the process from a neighbor lady, Anna Wesanen. Not only is my first name the same as hers, but I make my rugs the same also."

Lassila's home in Mohawk is a small museum of her work. Her quilts cover the beds. Flowers and birds she has embroidered decorate the walls. Rugs she has made on four looms she owns cover the floors of her two-story home, built in 1911, when copper ruled the Keweenaw Peninsula.

Even in her getaway cabin, deep in the woods of the Keweenaw Peninsula, braided rugs she is working on cover the tables.

"Oh, I love the work I do," said Lassila, whose woven, three-foot-wide rag rugs reflect her Finnish heritage.

"This is hard work and you never get paid for what you put into it. But for heaven's sake, I'll be doing this till I die, or at least till my son's new house gets filled up."

A thick, heavy, braided rug more than covers the dining room table in Anna Lassila's home in Mohawk, in the Keweenaw Peninsula in 1990. Lassila gets some help from Lorri Oikarinen of Calumet, who is learning the art of rug making from Lassila. They are working together to tightly twist strips of fabric into long braids. The heavy braids are then sewn with strong thread onto the other braided pieces, forming a thick oval that grows bigger with the addition of each piece. The finished product is a strong rug with patterns winding around in an oval shape.

Clockwise from above, Anna Lassila has four looms in her home and makes good use of them. Her fingers fly as she works the strips of fabric into the warp threads on her loom in 1992. She does many other kinds of needlework and moves from one project to another with the ease of a skilled artisan. She takes advantage of the warmth offered by a piece she is crocheting as she works to finish it. Framed pieces of her embroidery hang on the wall in the background. Lassila is known almost as much for her embroidery as for her rug making. She does elaborate designs in vivid colors, such as these wildflowers she created in crewel embroidery.

Charlie Parish

fisherman

He has tried other jobs, but they just don't cut it.

"I like being out on the lake," said Charlie Parish, a 47-year-old American Indian who fishes Lake Superior the way his ancestors did.

From a 16-foot aluminum boat, Parish tends 300-foot-long gill nets, hoping to catch the fish who gave their name to Whitefish Bay. Often, he works with his younger brother, William, keeping watch on up to 50 nets at a time.

"Every now and then, we come in with a ton of fish in our boat," Charlie said. "But most times, we barely cover expenses." Whitefish bring 60 to 80 cents a pound; herring and salmon, 40 cents.

Parish has gotten used to the cold waters, though he admitted a few years have gone by since he's been swimming in Lake Superior.

He spends a lot of time in his boat, even when he's not fishing. "I like taking the watery routes when I have to go somewhere. I don't like crowds, and I don't like big cities. But sometimes it can get a little scary," he added, thinking back to a night in November 1975.

"My dad and I were a half mile offshore. One minute it was calm and the next minute the wind came howling in on us and knocked us over. We were unprepared; there was no warning.

"I swam to shore to get a line on the boat and my dad stayed in the boat to save the catch. I've never seen a storm like that since that night, and I hope I never do again."

The next day they discovered the gale had sent the Edmund Fitzgerald to the bottom only 30 miles from where they had capsized.

Parish was soon back on the lake. "I like what I got in life now," he said. "I like where I live, and I like what I do. I probably will be doing this till the day I die."

Charlie Parish's day starts just after sunrise. One spring morning in 1988, he casts off at a deserted beach at Pendills Bay, not far from his home near the eastern point of Whitefish Bay. "It's work and enjoyment. I like being out in the fresh air," he says. He keeps his boat along the beach, minus the motor, and loads up every morning. He heads out into the bay, leaving his pickup truck parked along the beach. Hours later, he unloads his catch and the motor and goes home. He cleans the fish and ices them down until the wholesale buyer arrives to pick them up.

Gill nets are named because of the way they trap the fish. The fish swim into the netting, their gills get caught, and they can't back out. Trap nets, on the other hand, are made of more tightly looped netting. When the fish swim inside the opening of a trap net, they usually can't find their way out.

Charlie Parish fishes to support his family. It's a full-time job — no breaks, no napping in the sun waiting for the fish to bite. The pace is set from the start, getting out at first light to beat the waves that build as the day grows old, and speeding as fast as the boat will go to where the nets are set. All day long, it's pulling the nets up — in Charlie Parish's case, a job done by hand — and removing the fish. He tosses back the sport fish he isn't allowed to take and keeps the others. Lake Superior is so chilly, even in the summer, that his hands and the seats in the aluminum boat get ice-cold. The fish he catches in Lake Superior in the morning often end up in Detroit or Chicago that night. But the work doesn't end when he sells the fish to the wholesaler in the evening. Above and at left, he works on a net. Nets must be removed from the lake and dried out often because they almost constantly need repair.

To another bufflehead duck — or even to a human — one of Jim Wicks' creations looks a lot like the real thing, especially when nestled in its natural element. The feathered effect is created by careful use of the carving knife and practiced handling of the paintbrush. It doesn't hurt to have a lifelong acquaintance with fowl, as the Michigan Department of Natural Resources retiree does.

Jim Wicks

duck decoy carver

"I hope to die with the chips in my pocket and the knife in my hand," said Jim Wicks. The Michigan Department of Natural Resources retiree whittles away his hours with chips of basswood and a carving knife, making hunting decoys.

He does his carving in a workshop across the road from his home on South Manistique Lake, near Curtis in the eastern Upper Peninsula.

Wicks, 60, started carving full-size decoys when he was 14. He became more involved with carving when he worked with fellow hunters in the early 1960s.

He has decoys representing 15 species of ducks to use when he goes hunting. "Ducks are as definitive as people. They won't land unless they see their own kind."

Still, Wicks said, "I don't even have to load my gun for a good time."

Wicks keeps more than 150 decoys in his garage. The rest he sells to private collectors.

He was surprised when one of his carvings brought in something more exotic than ducks and geese.

"A six-foot bald eagle once tried to pick up one of my ducks."

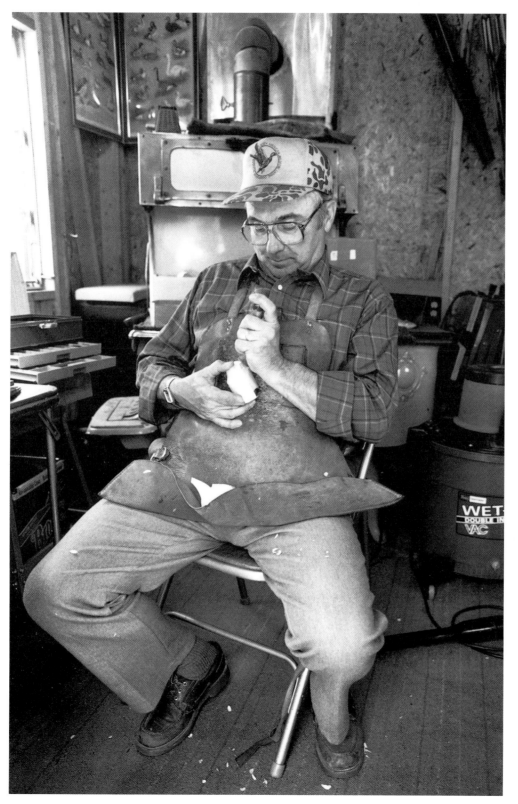

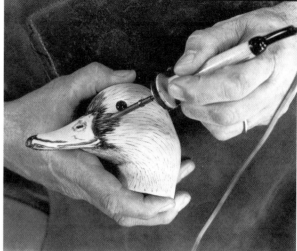

Jim Wicks carves a decoy in his workshop in 1988, letting the shavings and bits of wood fall on the floor around him. He and his wife, Marge, have wildlife scenes and symbols on the walls of their home, not far from his workshop. Marge Wicks shares her husband's love for the outdoors and recently began carving shorebirds. Above, Jim Wicks uses a wood-burning rod to darken the wood and create the feathered look for a male mallard decoy.

Toivo Reini

sauna stove maker

"In Finnish, Toivo means hope," said Toivo Reini (TOY-vo RAIN-y). With a twinkle in his eye, he added: "My parents gave me that name because they thought I was hopeless."

His mother and father came from Finland to the United States in 1911 and settled in the western Upper Peninsula, where he was born not long after they arrived.

For years, Reini has been building wood-burning stoves for saunas, the traditional Finnish heat baths that seem to sit in the backyards of almost all the homes in the UP.

"I wish I'd numbered them, but I haven't," Reini said of his stoves. "I don't really know how many I've made.

"When I was younger, I used to work in Detroit in the summer and winter up here in Ironwood.

"I guess I was a wrong-way Corrigan."

Eventually, he settled in the UP year-round. A back injury forced him to retire from farming and lumbering in the 1950s, and his family's farm was sold to make way for Gogebic County Airport.

"Money was getting a little tight. I was borrowing from Peter to pay Paul," Reini said. "So I started making these to help things out."

It takes him three days to make one stove. He cuts the iron, welds it, adds fittings for the water-holding tank and puts the stove together. "A guy that works fast can make it in two," said Reini.

"I don't care if I make much money. I don't want the business to get too big."

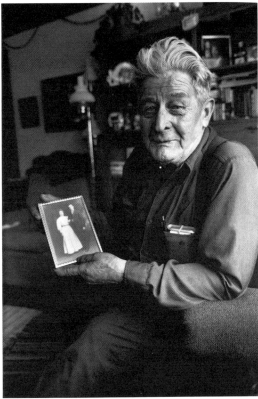

Toivo Reini of Ironwood makes sparks fly as he assembles a wood-burning stove for a sauna in the summer of 1992. The small furnaces must be able to endure years of intense heat, so they are made of heavy cast iron. For 30 years, Reini's stoves have provided the heat for the small buildings with tall pipes that seem to be in all the backyards in the Upper Peninsula, home to many descendants of Finnish settlers. Reini, 82, began making the stoves to supplement his earnings but the craft also gave him a better appreciation of his own Finnish heritage. Above, he holds a photograph of his parents at their wedding in Finland. They came to the United States in 1911 and settled in the UP.

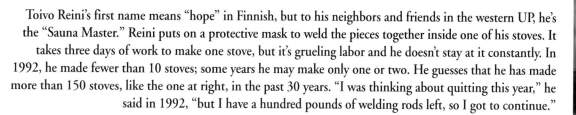

Toivo Reini's first name means "hope" in Finnish, but to his neighbors and friends in the western UP, he's the "Sauna Master." Reini puts on a protective mask to weld the pieces together inside one of his stoves. It takes three days of work to make one stove, but it's grueling labor and he doesn't stay at it constantly. In 1992, he made fewer than 10 stoves; some years he may make only one or two. He guesses that he has made more than 150 stoves, like the one at right, in the past 30 years. "I was thinking about quitting this year," he said in 1992, "but I have a hundred pounds of welding rods left, so I got to continue."

Sarah Turkey

black ash basket maker

A great Indian (Anishnabe) *leader named Black Elk knew his time was short. His people were restless; the Creator gave him a vision. Black Elk told his people to cremate his body and plant his ashes beside a pond. The morning after his ashes were buried, a tree appeared. His people protected it. When it matured, they cut it down and, as Black Elk had instructed them, pounded it until they had separated the growth rings from the trunk. Then they used the thin, striped pieces of wood to make* kokobinaganan, *or black ash baskets. And they learned patience.*
— Anishnabe *legend*

Sixty-three-year old Sarah Turkey didn't have the patience when she was young.

"My mom was doing some baskets, a few flowers, but not very much," said Turkey, an Ottawa Native American born on Manitoulin Island in Canada.

From childhood on, she worked the migrant farm labor camps from Michigan to Florida to New York and "all the places in between."

"When my brother got sick and thought he was going to die, he said to me, 'Come back here and I'll teach you everything I know,' " said Turkey. "So I went to him and I learned."

Now, she teaches the ancient art of weaving wood strips into baskets and other shapes at the Luce County Inter-Tribal Center for the Arts in Newberry. She asks that people bring "scissors, a jackknife and a will to learn."

… And patience.

Above, Sarah Turkey uses a small sledgehammer and a large knife to remove strips from a black ash log on the grounds of the center. Even the process of getting the wood ready takes a lot of time – and patience. She learned from her brother and now teaches people who come to the center so they can acquire the skills and pass the *Anishnabe* art to future generations.

Clockwise from left: Sarah Turkey sorts through the black ash logs that she keeps in a small pond so they won't dry out before she's ready to use them. The water keeps the wood supple. At her worktable, she finishes the top of one of her baskets. She also makes flowers and cattails, such as these, from the black ash tree. The little basket is in a traditional *Anishnabe* pattern, but the flowers and cattails are her own design. She makes large baskets and small ones; sometimes, she dyes wood strips red and green to make baskets that look like strawberries.

Bennett family

log haulers

What started as a family hobby grew into a part-time job for Melvin Bennett during his high school years.

Melvin put his family's Belgian horses to work pulling logs out of remote woodlots on the southeastern tip of the Upper Peninsula.

"It's a lot of fun," said Melvin, 18, who was an all-UP football player for DeTour High School in his senior year. "But it's a hard way to make a dollar."

The Bennetts have pulled a hundred-year-old page from the history of Michigan's logging camps. "They had to use the horses back then. They had nothing else," said Melvin, who is saving his income from log hauling for college.

The work has become a year-round affair for the Bennetts: Melvin's brother, Adam, 12, pitches in on the weekends; mom Karen, 40, and dad Ralph, 44, are both involved.

"Landowners don't want their land ruined by the heavy skidders some of the larger companies use," said Ralph. "They don't want the ruts in the land or the small trees backed over. They don't want the loss."

The Bennetts use the method proven during Michigan's lumbering heyday. Two of the family's Belgians are led into freshly cut woodlots. Pete is 7 years old and 1,900 pounds; Max is 6 years old and a mere 1,600 pounds. Huge logs up to 30 feet long are attached to the horses' harnesses. The logs are then dragged, one at a time, toward the waiting trucks for the trip to the lumber mills.

"This is a great hobby that's good for young horses," said Melvin, who hopes to become a veterinarian. "They learn real quick."

"The environmental damage of using horses is very, very slight," said his dad. "Plus, they fertilize the ground we're working on."

Above, Melvin Bennett guides Pete as the sturdy Belgian pulls him and a huge log out of a woodlot near Raber, in the eastern Upper Peninsula, in early 1992. Weighing up to 2,200 pounds, Belgians are as heavy as some cars and can easily haul loads that would stop other horses in their tracks. Belgians are 16 to 19 hands tall — or, from 5 feet 4 to 6 feet 4. Height in hands is measured from hoof to withers, the area at the top of the horse's shoulder. Belgians are among several breeds of draft, or work, horses and were bred in Belgium for heavy farm work. These powerful steeds are descended from the magnificent horses that armored knights rode into battle during the Middle Ages. At left, Pete stretches as Melvin Bennett collars him.

Ralph Bennett hooks Max's harness to a log and then guides him out of the woods, while Melvin leads Pete the other way. Pulling logs looks like material for a Currier and Ives landscape. But it is cold, hard work.

Pete savors a little revenge in front of the log-hauling truck that replaced his ancestors in the forests of Michigan.

Art Moilanen

It was way back last September, as far as I remember,
Walkin' the streets of Mass with lots of pride.
But I fell in the gutter and my heart is still a-flutter.
When a pig came by, it lay there by my side.
As I lay there in the gutter, and my heart is still a-flutter,
A Lady walkin' by had a chance to say,
"You can tell a man that boozes by the company he chooses,"
And the pig got up and slowly walked away.

— **"The Story of My Life"**
a song by Art Moilanen

For 60 years, Art Moilanen, shown in 1989, has been playing the accordion and singing the songs of his Finnish-American ancestors and their Upper Peninsula neighbors. He is 76 and lives in Mass City, in the western UP, where he entertains the residents of nearby senior citizen homes. He teaches his music and his style to apprentices.

Art Moilanen (MOY-la-nen) picked up his brother's accordion back in 1933 to learn the traditional songs of his heritage from his Finnish neighbors in the western Upper Peninsula. Soon, he began to write his own songs. Over the years, the tunes of the multiethnic immigrants to the UP blended with his Finnish sounds, and he created a new music that combines the stories, melodies and history of all the people of Michigan's north country.

Jingo Vachon

"During the boom days of our little copper mining hamlet, a lot of immigrants came here from Europe, especially from Italy, Croatia, Germany, Finland and Cornwall, England. Norway, Sweden and Poland contributed some, too. Language was a barrier, of course, because only the Cornish were adept with the English speech, but strange-sounding English it was for a fact! The mines were like Towers of Babel upside down."

— **"Finnish Fibbles"**
a book by Jingo Viitala Vachon

Jingo Viitala Vachon's (GING-oh VEE-tah-la vah-SHON) short, humorous tales capture the magic of life in the ethnic melting pot of Michigan's Upper Peninsula. Three books of her stories, "Tall Timber Tales," "Sagas from Sisula" and "Finnish Fibbles," bring the reader a pleasant view of growing up far from the city but close to the land.

Jingo Viitala Vachon, shown in 1989, has been playing the guitar, singing, and writing songs all her life. She loves to translate Finnish tunes into English and American songs into Finnish. She stands in front of the homestead her father built at the turn of the century in Toivola, southwest of Houghton. She was born in that house 75 years ago, the daughter of a Finnish immigrant who came to the Upper Peninsula to own land and live in freedom. He worked in the mines and fished before becoming a farmer.

Sleeping Bear Point

Leelanau County

Lake Michigan

Lake Huron

Mackinaw City

Petoskey

Alpena

Hubbard Lake

Lake Leelanau

Suttons Bay

Fairview

Grayling

Mio

Karlin

Higgins Lake

Arcadia

Skidway Lake

Baldwin

Clare

0 Miles 30

Northern Lower Peninsula

Kober shows his work in various stages. In his hand, he holds a finished trout, carefully painted to look real. In the middle is a piece of wood, with the shape burned in, all ready to be carved. Below that is a carving awaiting a paint job. "When I set in the eyes and the thing wakes up, when the fish looks back at me, I love it," says Kober, who is teaching the carving to his son, Travis, 18, and daughters, Heidi, 14, and Kelli, 11. "I hope to do this till the last day I breathe."

At right, Kober stands in the doorway of his workshop and studio in the spring of 1990. There are fish carvings everywhere — above the door, on the walls and used as the doorknob — as well as other reminders of the outdoors, such as the moose antlers above the doorway.

Dave Kober
fish decoy maker

Every time Dave Kober went fishing with his grandfather, he went home with a good catch — the tricks of carving decoys.

"When I was a little kid and would go spearfishing with my grandpa," Kober recalled, "he'd have me watching the hole for the fish while he sat there carving decoys. That's where I picked it up. I just started doing it alongside him, and over the years I just kept hacking away at it.

"I never went to a wood school," said Kober, 54, who now makes a living carving and painting fish decoys at his home near Arcadia.

Kober has made an art out of carving the traditional spearfishing decoy, a small lead-weighted, wooden lure suspended underwater on a short pole. From small bluegills — "I love those punky little bluegills; they're still my favorite carvings" — to a six-foot northern pike — "that one's swimming around somewhere in Austria now" — Kober has carved thousands of fish. "If it swims in Michigan, I've done 'em," he said.

Until six years ago, Kober worked for a construction firm that also specialized in toxic waste cleanup across the continent. He retired early and opened a small shop on a tree-covered hilltop a mile from Lake Michigan. "My carving got to be a full-time occupation," said Kober, "but I still enjoy it and I always will."

Although Kober's decoys are useful, especially for ice fishing, most never see water — or fish. "Ninety-nine percent of them sit on shelves," he said.

Clockwise, from bottom left: Dave Kober works to get the mouth just right on a fish. Because he pays careful attention to detail, his work is highly prized for its authenticity. Kober's carvings range from a few inches long to six-footers; they all require skillful use of tools and paints.

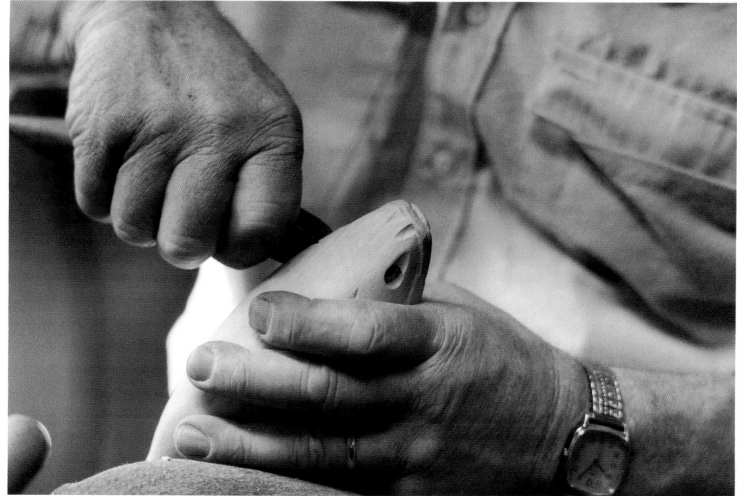

Three finished carvings, a pike, a trout and a sunfish — could pass for their nonwooden cousins swimming in the Great Lakes. Above, even the carver has to close up shop occasionally and go out after the real thing.

Donald Naganashe

quill box maker

"I try to do what was passed on to me by my grandma," said Donald Naganashe (NOG-ah-nosh), 45-year-old American Indian. "This is the only way I can enhance my feelings."

His grandma, Eva Mae Naganashe, would be proud. Naganashe carries on an old tradition and makes beautiful boxes using birch bark, sweet grass and porcupine quills.

"I'm doing this the way I was taught," Naganashe said. "Not just for sales. I am trying to maintain the ancient art form."

Naganashe travels within 100 miles of his home in Petoskey to gather the materials for his quill boxes. He starts by cutting a thin layer of bark off white birch trees. "A lot of people cut too deep and kill it," he said.

He then goes in search of sweet grass. The grass — found in out-of-the-way places — is used by Indians to add color and a slight, pleasant aroma to traditional tools and items made for the home.

He uses a tiny needle-like awl to thread the grass onto his boxes. Then he goes after porcupine quills, picking up carcasses along northern roads and hunting them when he has to. "You can get over 5,000 quills off three porkies," he said, "but you can't use them all."

After cutting the birch bark into small pieces to form the tops, sides and bottoms of the boxes, Naganashe works the quills into the bark with the awl. Using the natural shading of the quills, sometimes enhanced with bright colors, Naganashe creates patterns his grandmother taught him. "When people look at my work, I want them to know they're looking at a lifetime of heritage."

Donald Naganashe periodically visits fields far from his home to cut long blades of sweet grass to use in his quill boxes. It distresses him that some people pull the grass out by the roots, destroying the plants, which Indian people hold in high regard. Harriet Shedawin, a Chippewa Indian who lived at Sault Ste. Marie, had the same respect for sweet grass as Naganashe. Shedawin, who died in 1991, told of an Indian legend that says sweet grass never again will grow on any spot where it has been taken and used with disrespect.

Donald Naganashe teaches fellow Indians how to make porcupine quill boxes — if they want to learn in order to pass on the tradition, but not if they want to do it to make money. Winona Naganashe, Donald's 22-year-old daughter, is one of his students. In the picture at left, she is pushing a porcupine quill through a hole she has made in a piece of birch bark that will become the top of a box. On the opposite page is a finished box made by her father in a floral pattern. His boxes range from three to 10 inches in diameter. Dyes from natural sources, such as berries, were available even to his ancestors. Here, Donald Naganashe uses a sharp knife to cut only the thinnest layer of bark from a birch tree in 1992. He usually goes out for bark in midsummer and takes enough to last for a year, being careful not to cut too deeply so the tree won't be harmed. Woodlots where birch may be cut are getting hard to find. Naganashe cuts only with permission.

Clockwise, from lower left, the best artisans are able to choose quills of nearly identical length and thickness and fit them into the bark so that there is no space between them. The quills must lie smooth and flat with the colors forming the desired pattern. That isn't easy because the colors vary widely even if the quills are not dyed. From tip to base, the shadings range from black to brown to tan to white. First, quills are separated according to size and color on Donald Naganashe's worktable. The starburst and checkerboard patterns (pictured with blades of sweet grass below the boxes) were taught to Donald Naganashe by his grandmother.

Catherine Baldwin

quill box maker

Catherine Baldwin uses one of the scariest things in the forest to produce one of the most beautiful art forms of the Great Lakes Indians: porcupine quill boxes.

"I can't go to the store to get what I need," said Baldwin, an Ottawa Indian from Suttons Bay in Leelanau County.

She was referring to the quills, birch bark and sweet grass she uses to create the boxes.

Baldwin, 58, started quill work as a child. "Things are best learned at home," she said. "If a little kid wants to learn how to cook, she watches her mom. That's how I learned how to make the boxes, by watching my mom.

"I draw all my own patterns," said Baldwin. "Animals, floral, birds — whatever I feel like. Who's to know what's traditional nowadays? The art itself is a tradition.

"This is my hobby. I can work on it when I want to, and I can leave it when I want to." Her work sells at art galleries in northwestern Michigan for "a pretty good amount," she said.

She was at a loss to estimate the time it takes her to make a box. "I just do it. If I kept track of the work it takes to make these, I'd get discouraged," she said.

"This work takes a long, long time and a lot of sincerity. It's something you really got to want to learn."

Baldwin has taught the art form to her neighbor and friend, Kathryn Anne McGrath, so that their Ottawa heritage will live on.

"A lot of people came up to me and wanted to learn but Kathryn had the sincerity, she was the only one who carried a real sincerity to learn how to make the boxes."

Catherine Baldwin keeps the porcupine quills in water and then in her mouth so they bend easily when she pokes them through the birch bark. Below, she holds a tiny maple leaf alongside a drawing she has made of the leaf to be used as a design for one of her boxes. Among the Ottawa and Chippewa, quill boxes are places to keep treasured mementoes.

Jay Stephan

Au Sable boat builder

Jay Stephan (STEFF-on) is the fourth generation of his family to build the sleek craft known as Au Sable (AWE SAH-bull) River boats.

"My great-grandfather, Peter, came here from France in 1879," said Stephan, who has been making the boats for the past 30 years.

"He started out as a farmer but couldn't make it so he became a commercial fisherman and called himself a 'fishing farmer.' "

The boats have been used since the late 1800s to fish in the swift currents of the Au Sable, one of the nation's premier trout streams. Stephan, 67, spends about 200 hours building each boat in the workshop at his Grayling home, handcrafting from wood the long, flat-bottomed beauties.

"I wanted a boat for myself," said Stephan. "I've tried to build myself a fancy one, but somebody always comes along and buys it before it's finished.

"These boats are made for a lazy river like the Au Sable," said Stephan. "They're long and narrow and make a good platform to sit on. It's a lot better than wading because you get a lot less tired."

Out on the river, a guide sits in the stern and maneuvers the boat to place the angler in the best position.

Thirty-six of the 37 boats Stephan has built have stayed on the Au Sable River; his daughter Cheryl is helping him on his 38th.

And the family tradition won't end with her. "I bet she'll pass it on to her little ones."

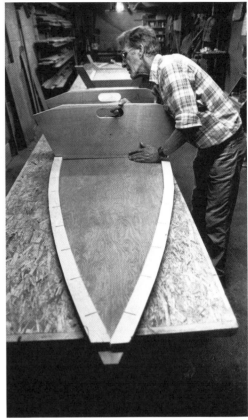

Without passengers or any other weight to balance him, Jay Stephan stands on the edge of one of his Au Sable River boats to demonstrate its remarkable stability. He steadies himself with the pole that he uses to help guide the boat down the river. Above, in his workshop, Stephan installs braces for the seats (like those pictured at left). The boats are so well-designed for the Au Sable that they actually do go with the flow, with only a little help needed from the pole in pushing off and correcting the course.

At top left, Jay Stephan holds the side of one of his boats to show how shallow they are. At left, he lines up braces along a floorboard. Above right, Stephan acts as a river guide while Jim Ritter of Grayling fishes for trout on the Au Sable in 1987. The river is so swift that chains, shown above at Stephan's feet, are needed to slow the craft down. Stephan releases many fish, but not all. "If I catch enough for dinner, I've had a good day," he says.

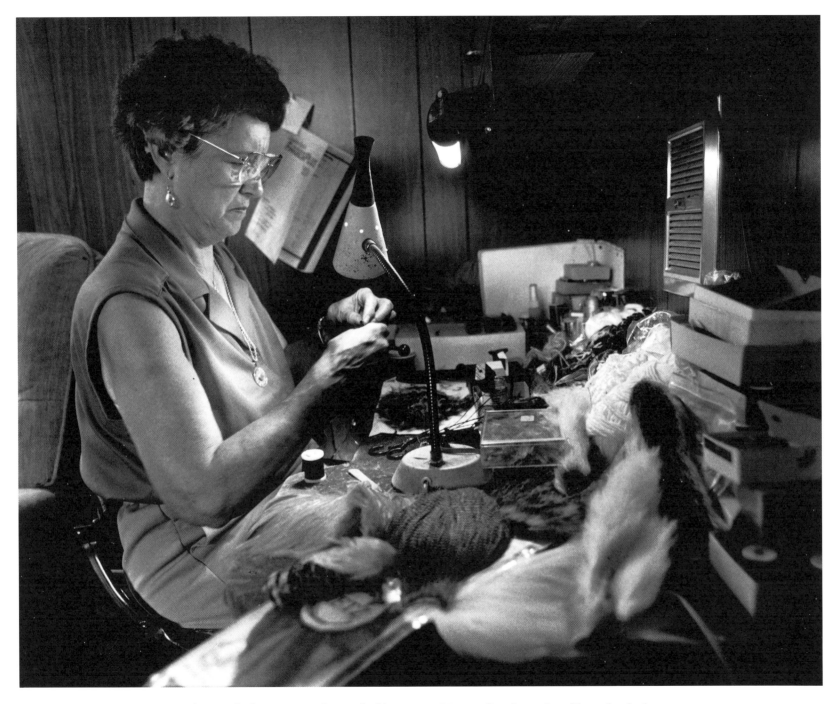

Josephine Sedlecky-Borsum at her worktable in 1987. Her supplies clutter the table — fur, feathers, yarn, floss and ordinary sewing thread. During the years when she ran Ed's Sport Shop in Baldwin, she tied flies in a corner of the living room of her home, which was attached to the shop.

Josephine Sedlecky-Borsum
flytier

With a hook, a strand of floss, some rooster neck feathers and a few turns of thread, Josephine Sedlecky-Borsum can convince the wary trout of the Pere Marquette River that a delicious insect is floating past them.

Sedlecky-Borsum, 75, has been tying trout flies — and fooling fish — for more than half a century.

"I love being out there on those streams," said Sedlecky-Borsum, who ran Ed's Sport Shop in Baldwin for 47 years. "When I was a kid I started tagging along with my older brother, John, and he'd take me out fishing.

"When I got married in 1937, my first husband got me started on fly-fishing and I really enjoyed it," said Sedlecky-Borsum.

"I'd go out fishing four or five nights in a row and the fish wouldn't take the flies I had, so I'd run back home and start making different ones until I'd find one they liked."

Sedlecky-Borsum created five new flies to try to fool the trout into the frying pan — the Lady Jo Caddis, Top Hopper, Baldwin Bomber, Tan Fury and Killer.

"On those really nice days I'd close down the shop, grab my rod and reel and head on down the Pere Marquette or take a few days off and run the Pine," said Sedlecky-Borsum. She still goes out fishing fairly often after supper.

"I've slowed down a bit now that I'm getting older, but I still make a few flies. Friends will pop in and say 'Jo, will you tie me a fly?' and I'll do it.

"There's no computer yet that can make them."

Sedlecky-Borsum cuts the thread from a newly tied Killer, one of her own designs. She can tie a dozen flies an hour. Her favorites are the ones that catch fish. Some flytiers are so serious about fooling the fish that they will pack small flytying kits in their fishing vests. While out in the stream with their fly-fishing rods, they take note of which bugs are luring the fish to the surface in hopes of a tasty meal, then quickly tie a fly that looks like the fish food.

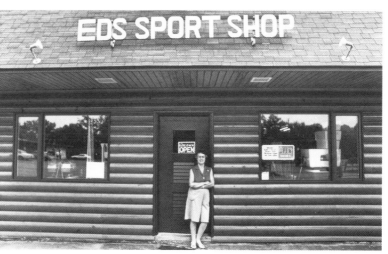

Bud Stewart works in the garage of his Alpena home in 1987. The egg cartons are for storing his carvings. Opposite, he wears a
lure around his neck. Sometimes he gets up in the middle of the night with an idea and starts carving. He uses an array of
paints and brushes to get the natural look.

Bud Stewart

lure maker

"Tell you what," said Elman (Bud) Stewart, "if you can't catch a fish, maybe it's too hot, too cold, too sunny or too cloudy.

"Maybe he's sitting at the bottom of his hole with a full tummy. Maybe he's too tired to move. Well, you take this lure and cast it over his home. He'll see this lure sticking its tongue out at him, and …" — Stewart showed his secret weapon — "he'll get real mad and come up to take a bite out of him.

"Bingo, you got your supper!"

Stewart, 81, has been telling some of the best fish stories in Michigan — and making lures — since he was 14. As a child, Stewart had a hard time finding the proper bait for his fishing trips. "I was out fishing one time and saw a baby muskrat go swimming by in a straight line, then it cuts fast to the side and, bam, a northern pike comes up and grabs him," Stewart remembered.

"I went into a bait shop looking for a muskrat bait and the guy threw me out. 'Pike don't eat muskrat,' he says. Heck, I just saw one do it. So I went home and started carving one."

Stewart turned professional lure carver when he was 17 and it kept him so busy he didn't finish high school until he was 20. Stewart also worked as a fishing guide, hunting guide and trapper. In 1980, Stewart retired from the commercial lure business but soon started carving decoys for collectors. He began repainting old wooden lures and earned enough to publish a book on his work.

Stewart enjoys trying new tricks. He made a fishing lure out of a golf ball, using a golf tee for the nose. "If it didn't catch a fish for you," he said, "maybe you could use it to try for a birdie."

Frank Ettawageshik

potter

When Frank Ettawageshik (etta-wah-GHEE-shik) strolls through the north woods, he takes out more than he brought in.

"This stuff is pretty valuable to me," said the Odawa (oh-DAH-wah) Indian from the Grand Traverse Bay area, "and it's worthless to others."

Ettawageshik, 44, was referring to clay and pulverized granite, gifts of the Earth with which he re-creates the traditional pottery the woodland Indians stopped making hundreds of years ago.

In 1973, Ettawageshik began teaching pottery at the Keweenaw Bay Indian Tribal Center in Baraga. He wanted to teach the techniques of his students' ancestors but could find no one who knew the methods. So he copied traditional pieces in the stoneware style he knew.

Since then Ettawageshik has removed all modern tools and devices from his Indian pot making, while his wife, Mary Ann, has taken over the stoneware style for their store, Pipigwa Pottery & Gallery in Karlin.

"The essence of the whole thing is the process," Frank Ettawageshik said, "being one and one with the Earth and the materials of the Earth."

When he leaves the woods, with his bags full of granite, clay and wood for the fires, he turns back and says *megwetch* (ME-gwetch), which means "thank you" in the language of his people.

Frank Ettawageshik searches through a quarry in 1987, looking for granite so old that it crumbles. With permission of the property owners, he takes what he needs, grinds it into sand-like particles and mixes it with clay. Opposite, he forms pots in the living room of his home adjacent to the store he and his wife run in Karlin. He sits underneath a portrait of his father. Ettawageshik's methods are as close to those of his ancestors as he can make them. He uses knotted vines and roots to make designs and uses his fingers to pinch the pots to even out the thicknesses. He fires the pots outdoors, using heat from burning wood. Everything he uses comes from the woods.

At left, one of Frank Ettawageshik's finished pieces, a small pot with a decorative pattern.

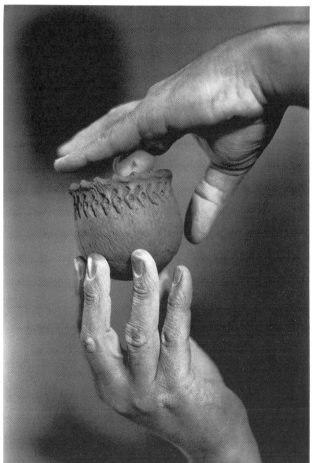

Edith Bondie

black ash basket maker

"We didn't learn it from anybody," said 75-year-old Edith Bondie.

"My mom made baskets and she'd throw us kids the scraps. We'd pick 'em up and play with them and started making baskets on our own. And I've been making them all my life."

Edith Bondie was born and raised on a Chippewa Indian settlement — "it really didn't have a name" — near Oscoda. "We'd make the baskets to play with, and in the summertime we'd sell them to the resorters — sometimes for a whole nickel."

Bondie lives north of where she grew up, on property her grandfather owned in Hubbard Lake. She has drawn from her heritage to create her own unique and beautifully detailed baskets, which she calls porcupine baskets.

"I kind of get a picture of something and try to create it," she explained. "You know that ocean fish that blows itself up a lot — the blow fish? It looks like a big balloon with lots of little needles all over it. Well, that's what the baskets are supposed to look like."

Strips of black ash wood must be trimmed to proper size and thickness, one by one, to insure an exact fit in Bondie's complex design. It can take her up to six weeks, working eight to 10 hours a day, to finish one basket.

"It's just my thing," said Bondie. "It's better than sitting around watching TV and doing nothing put pestering the neighbors.

"I wanted to quit making baskets a year ago. I want to spend time with my grandkids, but people still coax me into making them," she said.

"So now I'm teaching my good friend, Joyce Gardner, everything I know so that when I give it up she can take it over and teach."

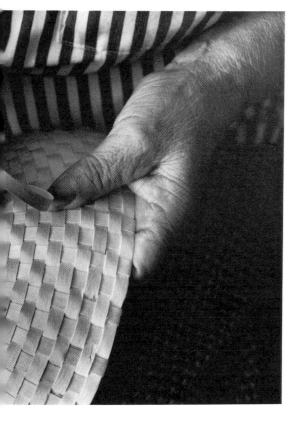

Edith Bondie calls her creations porcupine baskets because of the spines that she designs to protrude from the surface, just as quills poke out from a porcupine's body.

Edith Bondie prepares strips of wood for basket making in the laundry room of her home in Hubbard Lake in 1988. Pieces of wood lie all around in various stages of work. She uses a knife to strip the pieces down to the proper width and thickness so they will be pliable enough to work into basket shapes. When she has trimmed and stripped enough pieces to make a basket, she moves to her living room to finish the work. Because her style is so elaborate, it can take weeks for her to make just one basket. Most of Edith Bondie's baskets are used for decoration.

Elwood Henry

wood carver

Elwood Henry started carving when he was about 8 years old.

"My father used to teach us different things," said the 67-year-old Chippewa Indian. "When I carved a little animal and I'd get stuck, he'd come over and help.

"I've always liked doing it just for the fun of it."

Henry's lessons began shortly after his family returned to Michigan in 1933 after living for several years on the Indian reserve in Ontario where Henry was born. They farmed for a while near Skidway Lake before moving south, to the Saganing Reservation outside Standish. Henry continued with his carving as he grew up. He stayed with it as an adult, living on the reservation and working in construction.

When an injury forced him out of construction work, he began carving full-time.

He and his wife, Mille, retired and moved to Skidway Lake a few years ago, and the carving tools went with them. Now, back in the north woods near his childhood home, he makes moccasins, bear claw necklaces, pipes, dream catchers (free-form weavings of grass or rawhide made to block the evil spirits that turn beautiful dreams into nightmares) and other traditional Indian works of art.

Henry still makes the carvings he learned from his father, more to keep his heritage alive than to make money.

"I still like doing it because it's still fun," said Henry. "When you start out with a plain block of wood, it's not very much fun, but as it takes shape I really start to like it.

"I think it's a gift from God," said Henry. "I think you're just born with it."

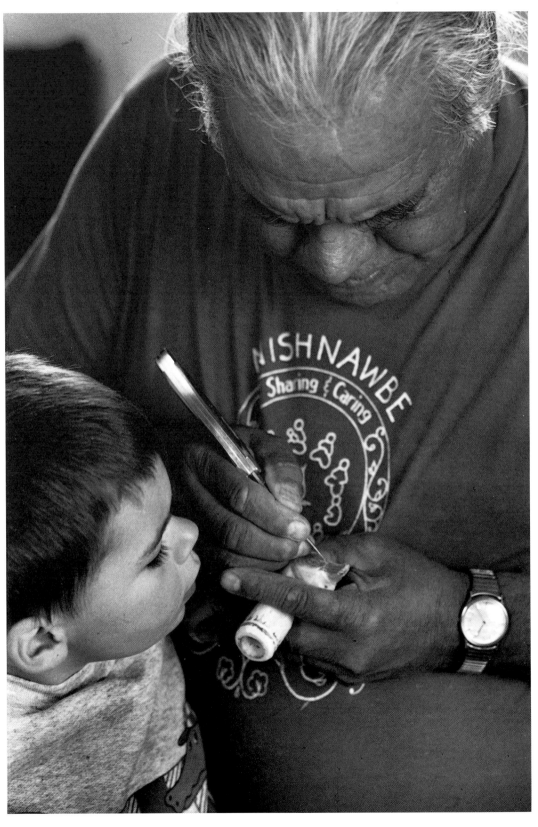

Elwood Henry carves a pipe in 1987 as his grandson, Michael Tremble, then 4, watches. Michael is now 10. Above, a miniature teepee and canoe made from sweet grass and birch bark are typical of the small pieces Henry makes. Years ago, when he was traveling to and from powwows to demonstrate his work, he sometimes traded the small carvings for gasoline. He has no idea how many small carvings he has done. Once he even carved a chess set.

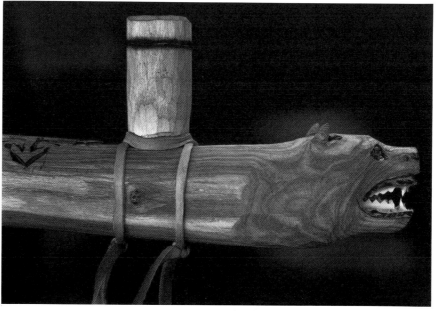

"It's a lot better than biting your nails," says Elwood Henry of his carvings. At left, he wears a necklace he made of bone and bear claws. Above, Henry and young Michael walk toward Henry's home on the Saganing Reservation in 1987. Even though totem poles are not associated with Great Lakes tribes, Henry put up a totem pole because "people who see movies think all Indians have totem poles." The peace pipe shows the detail of Henry's work. The bowl is made of ash, the pipe is sumac and the bear's teeth are cherry.

Damien Lunning

trapper

"When you're after coyote," said Damien Lunning, "you don't see many people. You do see a lot of empty traps."

Lunning, 51, is a professional trapper who works the woods around Mio, where he has lived all his life.

He started trapping as a boy. "There was nobody else around. No little kids to play with, but there were some traps around the house, and I taught myself how to use them."

Lunning began trapping coyote and fox for bounties back in the 1950s, when the state still offered them: Coyotes brought $15 for a male and $20 for a female, and a fox was worth $5. "It was a way to make some money," he said.

Lunning's wife, Judy, 48, helps with the trapping and does most of the skinning. They have added raccoon, otter, beaver, skunk, muskrat, weasel, opossum and mink to the list of animals they trap over a seven-county range.

The Lunnings used to sell the pelts of beaver, skunk, coyote and other animals to Hudson's Bay Co., which started shopping for furs in North America back in the 1600s. Fur isn't in demand the way it was a few years ago, but the Lunnings sell more than the hides. Scent glands are used in making lures for bow hunters and ingredients in perfume. Now, the Lunnings do most of their trapping for landowners who want to get rid of nuisance animals.

Above, Damien Lunning sets a trap in 1987. He baits several hundred traps in a seven-county area around his home in Mio. At right, he puts a skunk into his truck.

Usually working by himself, Lunning covers more than 200 miles a day checking his traps. Above, he walks into the Mack Lake area early in the day to inspect three of them. While making his daily rounds, he wears a belt with tools, a canteen and sprays that are used on the traps to attract animals. To cover his scent, Lunning crumples spruce and cedar cuttings and wipes them over his clothes. He never wears cologne or anything else that would alert animals to a human's presence. Damien Lunning is working with the Michigan Department of Natural Resources to help preserve bobcats in Michigan. He livetraps them, records their condition and releases them. He plans to stick with his trade. "It's my whole life. I ain't paid too much into Social Security, and I don't know how to do anything else."

Fred Litzner

walking historian

"I try to get family histories together," said Fred Litzner. "I like them to know their people."

Fred Litzner is a real walking historian. For years, he has been traveling northern Michigan with a bag full of books and papers about history. He talks to people, looks things up in libraries, and helps families learn about their ancestors.

Sometimes what he uncovers is spicy. He found a picture of a man who had three wives; his descendants are all over northern Michigan. He was a Mormon. Then there was the man who had two wives. He was pursued so intently by a pair of sisters that he married them both and kept them on different islands southeast of the Soo. He wasn't a Mormon.

Litzner follows his curiosity. Often, as he pores over old letters he has purchased, he makes a connection. Sometimes he just gets a chuckle. "One man wrote the Pullman Company that he lost his nightshirt in the Pullman. They wrote back and said they didn't know where it was."

Litzner farmed and worked in construction downstate and in mining out West before returning to the shores of the Straits of Mackinac, where his Prussian grandfather settled in 1885. "My father was 3 years old then and they would come across the straits with a horse and sleigh."

Litzner, 80, spends more time in his rented room in Mackinaw City than he used to, but his mind still travels nonstop. Recently, he had 300 prints made from a tintype so several people could see what their ancestor looked like.

"There are are so many families. There's no end of it, is there?"

Fred Litzner hasn't owned a car for years, so he walks or hitchhikes on his rounds to libraries. Folks gladly give him a ride for the chance to hear about what new project he's researching. At right, he walks up the path to the Chippewa County courthouse in Sault Ste. Marie in early 1991 to go over old records. Litzner's cane has been so well used that it's five inches shorter than an identical twin he bought at the same time years ago. Litzner wants to retire his old cane but can't get used to the other one. "I tried but it's a little high."

Sewing circles
quilt makers

Quilting pulls fabric and people together. As the women of Michigan's church sewing circles work, their good deeds circle the globe.

Members of the Fairview Mennonite Church in Oscoda County get together on the first Thursday of each month to sew quilts to sell at an auction, the Northern Michigan Relief Sale, held every August at the Oscoda County Fairgrounds west of Fairview. "We use the money for the needy, to feed the poor around the world," said Donna Esch, 75.

In Lake Leelanau, the quilters of St. Mary's Church meet Tuesdays and Thursdays to piece together quilts to sell to support the parish school.

All over Michigan, a domestic art that began as a necessity — the need to create warm bedclothes for cold Michigan winters — is warming people's hearts. In designing their quilts, Michigan's modern quilters get inspiration from each other and from sewing books and stores. They use traditional patterns and make new ones by mixing and matching.

The Michigan Quilt Project, begun by Michigan State University Museum, has created an archive at the museum in East Lansing with photographs and histories of nearly 7,500 quilts.

"Not only are these quilts beautiful, but they have a wonderful story to tell us about their makers," said Marsha MacDowell, curator of folk arts at MSU Museum. "The quilt may have been a gift to remember a birthday, a wedding ceremony or a family history. We want to create and maintain a record of the quilters, so the quilts don't become anonymous objects."

Esch, of the Mennonite sewing circle, said "If you get one of our quilts, nobody's going to have anything like it."

Above, in the summer of 1987, Donna Esch works at her dining room table on a quilt in the flower basket pattern. At right, she points to a removable heart pinned to Fairview on a wall hanging she quilted. The state's county lines form the quilt pattern on her map of Michigan.

At top, three women from the Fairview Mennonite Church work on a quilt in 1987. The pattern is Dresden plate, a design especially popular during the 1930s. Below, the women work on a quilt in the bear's paw or bear's foot pattern representing the harsh life of Michigan's pioneering families. Opposite page, women of St. Mary's Church in Lake Leelanau display quilts they made to support the church school in 1990. Clockwise from top, the patterns are: always friends, also known as badge of friendship, charm quilt, jigsaw and mother's oddity; log cabin; grandmother's flower garden; Kansas dugout; and embroidered rose wreath.

"Quilting is a significant historical and current activity," says Marsha MacDowell, curator of folk arts at Michigan State University Museum. "It's something that has not died away. If anything, the activity has strengthened over the years."

Christena Graves, 77, from Deckerville in Michigan's Thumb, is a good example. She has made more than 2,000 quilts since she was told in 1945 that she was too old to get a job.

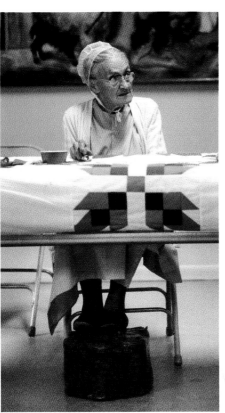

'Friendship and accomplishment'

"Mother's happiest times quilting were when she was in her seventies. She worked with a Church Group at this time. It was the third group of quilters to do this work and donate the proceeds to the Church. Some members pieced tops, others put together embroidered blocks other church members made. After the quilt was assembled and pinned to the frame the quilting began in earnest. The women met once a week during the winter months for several years (1970-1978). The most profitable work as far as church funds were concerned were the tops brought to the group to be made into completed quilts for the person who had treasured the top for many years. This time of friendship and accomplishment was a very happy experience.

"… As I said, we did not keep track of the number of quilts mother (Emma Consuelo Cramton-McQuiston) made but she gave one to each of her five children; to her 13 grandchildren; to her 12 great-grandchildren and to nieces and cousins and friends. She also made innumerable baby quilts that she sold at senior citizen craft fairs and she always had one ready to give to new babies among her friends and relatives."

Elvadolis McQuiston Johnson of Midland wrote this letter in 1986 for the Michigan Quilt Project of MSU Museum. Her mother, who was from Poseyville, just south of Midland, died in 1983. The letter is in MSU Museum and is part of "Michigan Quilts: 150 Years of a Textile Tradition," edited by Marsha MacDowell and Ruth D. Fitzgerald and published by the museum in 1987.

Don Perry

lathe turner

Don Perry goes on long walks through the north woods of Michigan, looking for pieces of bird's-eye maple and pieces of birch. He hunts for honey locust and Osage orange; thick, woody stems of lilac bushes; and black walnut.

"Black walnut is the most beautiful wood in the state," said the 74-year-old retired draftsman, who works with more than 90 species of wood.

"Walnut is how all wood is judged," he said.

Perry takes the pieces to the workshop at the back of his Higgins Lake home and carves them into finely turned bowls and dishes, Christmas tree ornaments, rolling pins and children's playthings. "I love to make toys for the kids," said Perry, who has four grandchildren and one great-grandchild. A minor stroke has slowed him down a bit but hasn't harmed his love for the craft or his eye for wood.

"My father set up a lathe in the basement when I was 9 years old," said Perry. "Anything that looked like it could be turned on a lathe, I'd turn it, until I blew out the bearings on my dad's lathe.

"He'd just go out and buy another; he'd rather me doing that than raising hell," said Perry. He also turns pieces of alabaster — hard-pressed, fine-textured gypsum found in Michigan — into vases and ornaments as translucent as fine china.

"Alabaster is very hard to work with," said Perry, who teaches others how to turn the stones. "A lot of the vases I started creating out of alabaster have turned into doorstops."

Don Perry sees the possibilities of good wood, even on a small scale. Above, in 1990, he stands in the doorway of his workshop with some tiny examples of his lathe work. The plate is made of finely polished wood that he fashioned from a piece he spotted in the forest. The tiny bottles, jars, bowls and vases are made of alabaster and wood and are typical of the toys he makes for his family. At left, the intriguing markings on his wooden sugar bowl are a result of the disease that caused the tree's death.

Alabaster, which is translucent when held up to the light, can easily be shattered during the cutting and shaping process. Perry, working in his undershirt in his back-room shop, salvages spoiled chunks by turning them into doorstops. At left, Perry turns a piece of alabaster on his lathe. Over the years, he has learned how to adjust the pressure so he can minimize the number of ruined pieces. The lathe creates so much dust that he uses one vacuum cleaner to pull the dust from the air and another to blow it outside. He has a ventilating fan above his worktable.

Two Amish girls ride their bicycles to school just north of Mio. Dozens of Amish families make their homes between Mio and Fairview in Oscoda County. An Amish community settled in the Mio area in 1900, but the population had dwindled to virtually nothing by 1954. Amish families resettled there around 1970, and the community is thriving.

The Amish

a way of life

"And be not conformed to this world."
(Romans, 12:2)

"And be clothed with humility: For God resisted the proud, and giveth grace to the humble."
(1 Peter, 5:5)

Traveling through modern Amish (AH-mish) districts is like driving through a living museum. Little has changed since the first Amish settlements in Michigan were founded in 1895.

The Old Order Amish Mennonites are followers of Jacob Amman, a 17th-Century Mennonite bishop who evangelized strict interpretations of the Bible. The Amish shun modern technology and strive to maintain a simple life-style.

Horses and bicycles are their transportation, wood and coal their sources of heat. Electricity is unwelcome in the homes of the people whose way of dressing — broad-brimmed hats and black pants with suspenders for the men and long, unadorned dresses and head coverings for the women — removes them from the shopping malls of the 20th Century.

Close to 5,000 Amish in 25 communities across the Lower Peninsula now call Michigan home. Reasonable land prices, freedom to teach their children and warm acceptance from neighbors have encouraged many of the practitioners of simplicity and family unity to move into the Great Lakes State over the past two decades.

"This is more than a religion," said Roy Yoder, 38-year-old Amish evangelist and wood craftsman from Ovid in the central Lower Peninsula. "This is a way of life."

Many Amish do not use electricity or other manufactured power. Some use electricity generated on their property, but most adhere to the old ways. Michigan Amish families are known for their steadfast adherence to family farming. Living in a few scattered Amish settlements in northern lower Michigan and south-central Michigan, they tend dairy herds, raise grain for their cattle, grow produce and raise poultry. The Amish family van is a buggy. Sometimes, Amish people will ask friends and neighbors to take them somewhere in a car, truck or van. But such instances are relatively rare. Supermarkets in Amish areas often have hitching posts. You can sometimes spot an Amish home by what is not there — a television antenna or utility wires.

It is important to Amish people to be free to educate their children in their own schools, such as this one, above, located north of Mio. In 1990, there were an estimated 30 Amish-run schools in Michigan. Children attend through the eighth grade. Their education continues as they learn a craft or a trade from their parents. In schools, as in Amish homes, simple living is stressed. In "The Amish in Michigan," from "Ethnic Michigan: A Tribute to Diversity" to be published by University of Michigan Press, author Gertrude E. Huntington points out that Amish schoolrooms are decorated with mottoes that make their point with humor, such as: "A smile is a curve that sets a lot of things straight," "To be contented with little is hard; to be contented with much is impossible" and "Walking fast doesn't help as much as starting on time." At right, a rare sight: An Amish girl in traditional dress uses a power mower to cut her family's lawn north of Mio.

On the first Saturday in May and at the start of the Labor Day weekend, Emanuel Yoder closes his blacksmith shop and turns his 20-acre farm east of Clare into a 300-stall flea market and auction site. Here, an Amish man and boy watch as horses and farm wagons are auctioned at the corral.

A young girl and her mother wear the long dresses and bonnets typical of the clothing worn by Amish women and girls. Although Amish women wear pink and blue, vivid colors such as red, yellow and orange are avoided. The mother and daughter are taking in the sights and sounds of one of the flea market-auctions held on the Emanuel Yoder farm near Clare in 1991. On auction days, horses, household goods and food are sold at the Yoder farm, with proceeds going to the Amish schools. The night before the auction, $5 lets buyers and sellers camp out on the farm and enjoy a pig roast and bean soup supper. They are asked to bring a cold dish of food to add to the potluck meal.

Two boys in traditional Amish clothing are miniatures of the adults as they discuss the pros and cons of the items offered by the auctioneer. Amish people from Michigan and neighboring states work together to set up the twice-a-year outdoor markets at Emanuel Yoder's farm. "The auctions keep on getting bigger every year," says Yoder's brother, Rueben, who comes up from Ohio to help. Emanuel and Rueben Yoder are not related to Roy Yoder, the woodworker from Ovid. Yoder and three other common Amish surnames — Miller, Bontraber/Borntrager and Hochstetler/Hostetler — accounted for almost half of the 263 households listed in a recent Michigan directory of Amish families.

Women in traditional Amish dress pass visitors in more contemporary attire. The auctions attract many people who are not Amish. Around 7 a.m. on market days, traffic starts backing up along U.S.-10 as browsers arrive. By noon, eight auctions are going on — for horses, farm machinery, tack, stoves, furniture, wagons, nails and handmade quilts, which draw the biggest crowds. "You've got to get here pretty early," says Roy Yoder, the Amish woodworker from Ovid, who sells his bentwood chairs at the auctions. "If you're not here early, you have to park in another county."

Sunset on an Amish farm near Mio: A farmer and his son unhitch their equipment while cattle graze in the field beyond and a horse with a buggy trots down the narrow lane.

Sunrise

Isabella County

Southern Lower Peninsula

Lake Huron

Lake Michigan

0 Miles 30

Mecosta ◆

◆ Mt. Pleasant

◆
Blanchard

Frankenmuth ◆

Flint
◆ ◆ Davison

Ovid ◆

◆ Dryden

East Lansing
◆

Marine City ◆

Lansing ◆

◆ Cohoctah

Dorr ◆

◆ Hastings

◆ Mason

◆ Hartford

◆ North Adams

Les Raber

fiddler

"I'm not a violinist," said Les Raber, "not by any stretch of the imagination. I'm a fiddler."

Lester Raber, a retired farmer who has called Hastings home for 64 of his 82 years, has been playing the fiddle since he was 10 years old.

"My grandfather was a good fiddler," said Raber, "but he had a stroke when I was growing up and I had to learn it all on my own. So I can only read a little bit of music.

"But if I hear it I can usually figure it out."

Raber played in seven different bands around Michigan, one of which played Friday nights at the Dixie Dance Hall in Wayland for 19 straight years. "We just never got a name for the band," said Raber.

"Now, all my playing is just for fun," Raber said. He plays every other week at jamborees organized by the Original Michigan Fiddlers Association, a small but dedicated group of musicians who work to maintain those old-time tunes that grew up with Michigan. Once a month, Raber plays at nursing homes.

He owns a few fiddles, but his favorite — which he still plays — was made out of mahogany in 1908 by Alex Flietz of Plainwell.

"I don't have any idea of the number of songs I've picked up over the years," said Raber, whose favorites are jigs, reels and waltzes. "But I'm always looking for a better one."

Les Raber, above, spends many hours with his fiddles in his living room. He likes to play alone because he feels free to develop his music to suit himself. He favors jigs and reels and other traditional tunes that hark back to the 19th Century in America. Although he prefers playing by himself, Raber is on the road a lot, traveling throughout Michigan to jamborees as far away as the western Upper Peninsula. He picks up new tunes and ideas by listening to other musicians. At left, he steals away from the crowds at a Battle Creek jamboree in 1991 and finds a quiet corner where he tunes up his instrument.

"I love the sound of the music. I like to play with my eyes closed so I can hear it better, so what I see doesn't detract from what I hear," says Russell Nelson, at right in one of his barber chairs in 1987. He is credited with helping to develop Michigan fiddle playing, a combination of musical styles identified with fiddlers from the Great Lakes State. Just as the sound of a voice can tell you where a person comes from, so can the sound of a fiddle.

Russ Nelson
fiddler

He learned how to play the tunes his father taught him on the fiddles his father made him.

And he kept fiddling around for the rest of his life.

"I grew up in Kalkaska," said Russell Nelson. "My father taught me how to play and made me a fiddle to help get me started.

"Then he ordered me one from the Sears catalog. I remember going down to the train station every day and waiting for the fiddle to arrive. That was a great day when it finally came."

Nelson played his first square dance when he was 9 and made his living playing on radio stations around central Michigan in the early '30s. He died in February 1990 at age 74.

"Russ had a knack about him," said his wife, Edith. "He played by ear. He would just hear a song and he'd pick it up, add a few of his little embellishments, and that was that."

After serving as a merchant marine during World War II and attending barber school in Detroit, Nelson opened Russ's Barber Shop on the south edge of Lansing in 1946. "When I opened the shop, I'd play the fiddle to pass the time between customers. When somebody came in, the fiddling would have to wait. But now," Nelson said in 1987, "the customer has to wait and the fiddling comes first."

Nelson played square dances and nightclubs in the Lansing area and helped establish the Original Michigan Fiddlers Association in 1976.

Nelson's son Douglas has picked up and played his father's fiddles occasionally. Douglas' 19-year-old son, Russ, "has a great knack for the fiddle," said his grandma, Edith. "I'll think he'll do a lot with it."

Clockwise, from top left, Nelson fiddles while his friends, Bob Emerson, Dorsey Lawrence and Howard Glossop, play along. The exterior of Nelson's barbershop gives no hint that just beyond the barber pole a concert of strings is in progress. Guitar polish, bows and a fiddle seem perfectly at home on a countertop made for shaving cream, a razor, combs, brushes and scissors, the tools of Russell Nelson's livelihood.

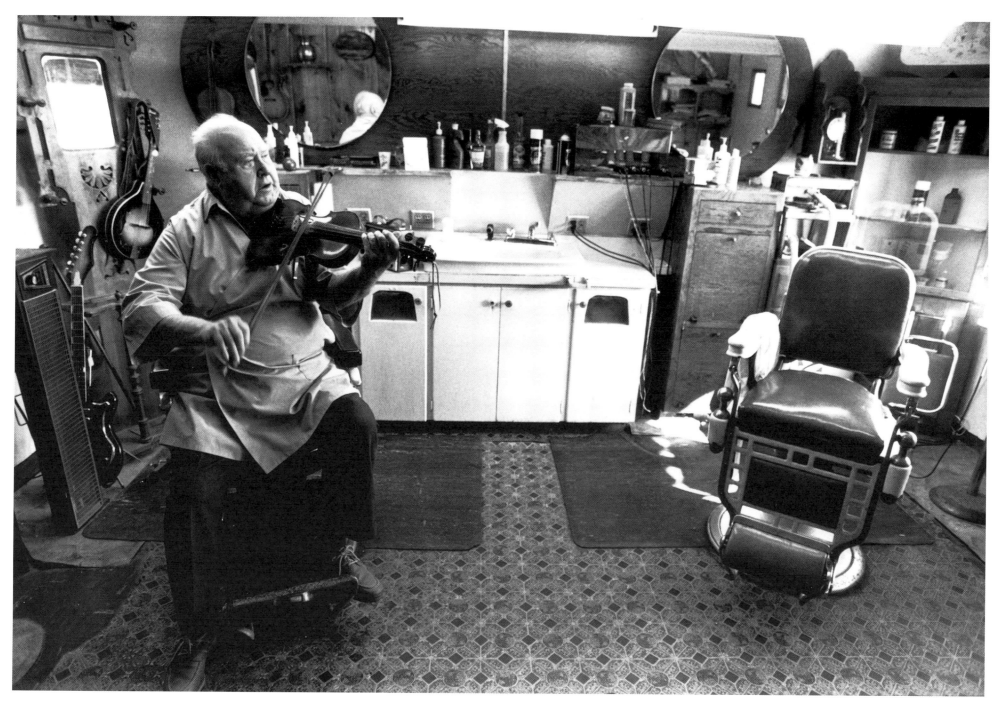

While Russell Nelson was practicing his craft with scissors and comb at the barbershop, he also was improving his talents on the fiddle, mandolin, guitar, banjo, bass, Jew's harp, piano and mouth organ. Above, with the shop empty one day, he tries out a tune. The other chair is open for someone who drops in for a haircut, but the customer might have to wait until the tune is finished. A slow day could find Russ Nelson picking up a few of his other instruments and fiddling around with them. That's a mandolin hanging up just behind him and an electric guitar propped up below that. Everything's ready, as usual, for Nelson's friends to stop by, choose an instrument or two and launch into a few impromptu jam sessions between trims.

Marie Cross

herbalist

When Marie Cross was growing up, a trip to the drugstore was a walk through the fields behind her grandparents' home near Mecosta.

"My granny would gather us together and say, 'We're going to go get our winter medicine,' " said Cross, whose roots in Mecosta County, about 50 miles northeast of Grand Rapids, go back to the mid-19th Century.

Before the Civil War, Cross' grandmother, 18-year-old Lucy Millard, fled her parents' home in Palmyra, Missouri, to search for the man she loved — Isaac Berry, a slave on a neighbor's plantation who had fled to Canada. They were reunited in Ontario and got married. In 1877, they moved their growing family to newly cleared farmland in Mecosta County.

"Isaac helped build this county," said Cross, 77, who lives within a mile of her grandparents' homestead. "He gave two acres of his farm for the first school in the area, and Granny Lucy was the first teacher.

"My mother died when I was 8 years old, and Granny came over to live with us," said Cross. "That's when I learned the herbs.

"I've doctored all my family with herbs," said Cross, "and my favorite one is the dandelion. My grandmother would roast the roots, grind them and make coffee. She would use the leaves for greens in salads and soups and as spring tonic and gallbladder tea. And you can make white wine from the blossoms or dip them in batter and roll them in sugar for delicious treats. Even as kids we would take the stems and make little curls out of them and hang them over our ears.

"Man may be trying to get rid of them, but God never intended the dandelion to die out."

Marie Cross gathers cuttings from an everlasting plant. They will be tucked into pillowcases to help bring sleep. Her grandmother taught her to see fields as medicine cabinets. "We lived mostly off the land — hunting, fishing, gathering. She taught us how to gather them and how to cook them. She taught us how to use things others call weeds. I think everybody grew up knowing what herbs would do for them back then. It was a necessity because of the lack of doctors."

Cross holds a mullein plant. It is eaten to soothe coughs; it is also used as a balm for hemorrhoids. Some of the medicinal teas Cross' grandmother taught her to brew are from alfalfa leaves, for pain in joints and to help digestion; watermelon seeds, as a diuretic and to relieve kidney and bladder problems; comfrey leaves, to soothe the stomach; chickweed, to induce sweating and help dieters; elderberry blossoms to reduce fever.

Cross hugs her great-granddaughter, Jessica Smith, then 3, in 1992. Jessica is learning the same lessons Cross learned from her grandmother, who was born before the Civil War. The treasures of the field aren't just remedies. At right, Cross holds red lichen used in potpourri.

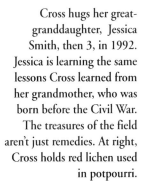

VanAntwerp family

cedar fan carvers

Glen VanAntwerp is carrying on a family tradition begun more than 100 years ago in the lumber camps of northern Michigan.

VanAntwerp, 43, a computer systems manager in Lansing, is following four generations when he carves elaborate fans and fan-tailed birds from northern white cedar.

His great-great-grandfather, John, brought his family to Michigan after the Civil War so he could work in the booming lumber industry. John's son, C.M., and grandson, Elmer, followed his example and went to work in the lumber camps, where the workers whittled away the long, cold Michigan nights.

Though the lumber industry dwindled, the whittling was passed on to Elmer's son, Stanley VanAntwerp, and Stanley's son, Glen.

"I'd watch Grandpa carve these cedar fans and thought they were just beautiful," said Glen. The carving is far from simple. A strong, sharp knife is needed to cut the fan blades, going against the grain of the cedar. The carvings are then soaked for an hour in boiling water so the fan blades can be spread out. The fans become the tail feathers and wings on the bird carvings; a wood-burning tool is used to darken the beaks and eyes.

The VanAntwerp tradition already has been passed on to a sixth generation. Glen has taught the art he picked up from his grandfather to his son, Jeremy, 22, and daughter, Sara, 17.

They learned the same way he did — by watching.

It doesn't take Glen VanAntwerp long to make one of his carvings, but it took him a long time to learn the skill that whittled away the hours in Michigan's lumber camps.

*The Lumberjack had naught to do
on long cold winter nights,
But sit beside the old wood stove
by lamp or candle light.
So some of them took to carving,
the things they made were fine.
Some of them made balls and chains
and some made fans like mine.*
— by John Smedley of Kewadin, who learned the art from his lumberjack father.

Near left, a cedar fan is spread out, revealing the detail in the carving. The VanAntwerps, far left, turn blocks of cedar into decorative fans and fan-tailed birds. Clockwise from left, Stanley; his son, Glen; and Glen's children, Sara, then 10, and Jeremy, then 15, show some of their carvings in 1986. Below, birds in various stages of completion are lined up alongside Glen VanAntwerp's carving knife on his workbench.

Herman Pieters, of St. Thomas, Ontario, watches as Keilhofer works on a statue of Jesus in 1988. Above, Keilhofer pays careful attention to detail in carving the cloak on the statue of Jesus. Below left, Keilhofer works on a bust of Martin Luther for Grace Lutheran Church in Redford Township. Keilhofer teaches several classes a week in his studio and holds carving seminars during the summer. "I like to teach the classes," says Keilhofer, "I like to bring out the talents some of the students don't even know they have." Keilhofer's largest statue, a 10-foot-3 Virgin Mary with Christ Child, was made for St. Mary's Catholic Church in Alma. Keilhofer learned carving after his father was declared missing in action in World War II. "My mother couldn't get any pension and we didn't have any money. So we had to find a way to make some."

Georg Keilhofer

wood carver

"I don't copy anything. I come up with my own designs and make a clay model instead of a drawing because it's a lot better. People can see what a relief sculpture would look like." Keilhofer, above, working on the Martin Luther statue, prefers oak but carves mostly basswood. He uses more than 140 gouges for his work. He produces statues, wall plaques, ceiling tiles, doors and entranceways. "I like to carve almost anything." Keilhofer has his own woodworking shop in Frankenmuth, Michigan's little Bavaria.

"I don't know if I'll ever retire," said Georg Keilhofer (kile-HO-fa). "I'll probably make my own casket and sit myself in it when it's time.

"I started carving school when I was 14," said Keilhofer, 59, who moved from Bavaria to Michigan a quarter century ago.

"Next to the Berufsfachschule Fuer Holzschnitzerei (the Trade School for Woodcarving, in Berchtesgaden) was the historical museum and they gave out homework to people who were interested. And so my mother and I, when I was 13 years old, we did doll furniture, all handmade. That gave me the idea to check with the school, the same school my father went to 30 years before me, to see if I could get in there."

Keilhofer took four years of carving and two years of cabinetmaking at the school, which started out teaching drawing in the 19th Century and switched to carving in the early years of the 20th. After graduation, he opened a cabinetmaking shop and refined his skills at the art practiced in Bavaria for hundreds of years.

His first visit to the United States in 1966 led to a full-time job. He moved his family to Frankenmuth and went to work as a carver in a cabinet shop in 1967. He started teaching that year, too. "I didn't know the English language very well and I needed a translator," said Keilhofer, "but I can get by without one now."

Dan Rapelje

pigeon racer

You don't need a map to find Dan Rapelje's (RAP-ill-jay) home in Lansing. All you have to do is look up. Large flocks of pigeons can be seen darkening the sky.

"They're just the young ones circling the loft, getting to know the area," said Rapelje.

He raises pigeons — not city types that leave their mark while sitting atop statues, but homing pigeons that race back to their lofts when released hundreds of miles away.

"The difference between the city pigeons and the birds I raise is the same as a plow horse and a thoroughbred," said Rapelje, who keeps more than 300 of the racing "homers."

"When my father passed away in 1980, my mother asked me, 'What we gonna do with dad's birds?'" said Rapelje, who lives next door to the house in which he was born. "I asked for the whole lot. 'I'm gonna fly them,' I said."

Since then, the pigeons have become a big part of life for the 58-year-old former truck driver. Before, Rapelje said, "I had my head in a bottle. Having these pigeons is good therapy. Through a lot of prayers and working with these birds, I don't have time for nothing else."

They begin competitive racing at 6 months. For short races of 120 miles, the birds start near Ft. Wayne, Indiana. Long hauls — 600 miles — begin near Athena, Alabama. The pigeons are released and timed. "We can measure the exact length of each bird's flight home, down to a thousandth of a mile," said Rapelje.

"A good bird with good weather will be home the same day it's released, but every now and then, one of them won't show up."

Dan Rapelje leans against the birds' main loft, named Jersey West F Troop. He says the inhabitants of F Troop make mistakes sometimes, just like the characters in the 1960s TV series. Above, Rapelje's homing pigeons in their cubicles inside the loft in 1992. He lets the birds mate three times; each mating produces two eggs. Their life expectancy is usually 14 to 16 years, but Rapelje has heard of some that live to be 26.

Clockwise from left, three of Rapelje's 300 or so pigeons hang out on their roof. Some of the lofts were built by Rapelje's father in 1948. Rapelje spreads the wings of a Husken Van Reial pigeon to show the bird's flying apparatus. The first three feathers are the power feathers for speed. The thick feathers below them are the secondaries, the ones that keep the birds in the air and help them coast. Pigeons aren't the only feathered creatures that get loving treatment from Rapelje. Here, he has a kiss on the beak for his pet parakeet, Petey. Rapelje's interest in pigeons is shared by people around the world who breed and train and race their birds for a hobby. The racing homers are from the family of rock doves or rock pigeons that have lived in the wild for thousands of years. Their fantastic ability to find their way back home made them useful to people as message carriers as long ago as 1,000 B.C. The birds were deployed by the U.S. military to deliver messages as recently as the 1950s.

Bernie Crater Snow family

syrup makers

The first days of spring bring smiles to our faces, flowers to our gardens and the sweetest of stories. Maple syrup.

The process hasn't changed much over the past three centuries. When the sun comes out and turns the short, cold days of winter into the gentle days of spring, syrup makers head into the maple stand, or sugar bush, and drill small holes into the trees. Spouts are inserted and buckets placed below them to collect the sweet water, or sap.

The buckets are emptied into a larger container and the sap is transported to the sugarhouse, where it is boiled in a large, shallow pan over a roaring fire, reducing the thin sap to syrup. Depending on sugar content, 25 to 50 gallons of sap are needed to produce one gallon of the best topping for pancakes and waffles, pure maple syrup.

Some archaeologists say the Europeans introduced syrup making to the American Indians in the early 17th Century, partly because the Indians didn't have the equipment needed to process the sap. But many archaeologists believe that through natural freezing and evaporation, and by adding red-hot stones to the sap in wooden vats, the northeastern Indian tribes indeed may have produced the sweet treat. The answer might never be found.

Bernie Crater and the Ralph Snow family are two of today's maple syrup makers in Michigan. The tools have changed a little but their syrup tastes the same as syrup made 350 years ago.

After years of working at Crater's with his twin brother, Eugene, Fritz Lehman knows the maple syrup process almost by instinct. Above, Fritz checks to see whether the steaming syrup is thick and sweet enough to be filtered. Bernie Crater, owner of Crater's Pure Maple Products in North Adams, holds up a pint of syrup to check for clarity. Syrup can be made from walnut and birch trees, but the sap doesn't flow as well and the sugar content is not as high. Because sun helps the maples convert nutrients into sugar for food, lots of bright summer days usually mean a good syrup season the next spring.

Bernie Crater, 69, outside of his sugar shack during the syrup season in 1988. The sugar shack used to be a barn behind the house where he was born. Far left, John Blakley, then 16, carries a bucket of sap to one of Crater's container wagons from a tree stand in Litchfield in 1988, while a small boy sneaks a peek at one of the taps. Crater taps trees for miles around North Adams, working it out with the property owners by donating money to local charities for every bucket he taps on their land. Michigan State University estimates the state has about 600 commercial syrup producers. The range is from about 50 gallons a year for the smallest ones to 7,000.

For the past 30 years, Ralph Snow has been carrying on a spring tradition his family started four generations ago — making syrup. "There's no money in the corn and bean fields anymore," Snow says. "Maple syrup is the thing that keeps me alive." Above, Mark Schaver empties a bucket into one of the Snow family's container wagons, which is then emptied into the Sap Wagon Express at right.

As the winter snows disappear, the Snow family takes to the woods. Three generations of Snows gather outside the family business as the maple syrup season gets under way in 1993. Ralph, 53, stands in the back, between his parents, Bertha, 71; and Monty, 78. From top left are: Ralph's daughter, Penny, 21; and Ralph's twin sons Mark and Matt, 19. Above, Brett Droscha loads wood into the evaporating tank inside the Snow family's sugar shack, where sap is slowly heated and turned into pure maple syrup. The family hangs nearly 5,000 buckets on the hard maples along the road and in the tree stands, or sugar bushes, of friends and neighbors in central Ingham County. "If we don't get there on time and hang our buckets," Ralph Snow says, "they start to think we're mad at them."

Yoder family
furniture makers

There are no posted hours on the small, hand-lettered sign that announces the location of his business. Just a note to let you know that Yoder's Hickory Rockers is "Closed Sundays."

"We don't have any set hours," said Roy Yoder, a 38-year-old Amish minister who started making the bentwood rockers eight years ago.

"It all just depends on the daylight. And if we get bored, we go fishing."

Yoder learned the Amish tradition in Ohio from his father-in-law, Roy Miller. After watching him at work for two days, Yoder purchased a chair from him and studied it.

"The only real way to learn it is to do it," Yoder said.

Son Merle, 15, starts by trimming the branches off saplings and sanding them. The young hickory trees are from 1/2-inch to four inches around and are purchased from the Yoders' Clinton County neighbors. Roy and Merle cut them to size and place them in a steam bath.

After two hours, the saplings are bent and left overnight in a jig to assume their distinctive curves.

While Roy and Merle put the chairs together, daughter Celesta, 14, sands the maple, walnut or cherry wood slats for the contoured seats and chair backs. Finished chairs are varnished and sealed by mom Mary Yoder.

"It's a family project," said Roy Yoder. "We like it because we can do it together."

Celesta sands a piece of maple on one of the family's rocking chairs in 1993. She is using a belt sander run by an air compressor used to power the tools in the small shop behind the family's home near Ovid, northeast of Lansing. The Yoders also make end tables and footstools out of hickory saplings and maple and walnut slats. The family is following an Amish tradition by learning and passing on the art of furniture making. Many Amish families in the Great Lakes area support themselves and provide for their own uses through carpentry and woodworking.

Clockwise, from above left, Merle watches as his father, Roy Yoder, places the hickory saplings in the steam bath to make them pliable enough to bend. Roy Yoder measures the slats for the back of one of his chairs. The bentwood rocker is an old-style design that offers full support and comfort because it is contoured to fit around the body. Roy Yoder measures a wood brace to make sure it will support the seat properly. The Yoders sell the furniture they make directly from their home through word of mouth and at the auctions which draw large crowds of browsers and buyers twice a year to an Amish farm near Clare.

Near right, two of the Yoder family's rockers, with cut hickory saplings lying on the ground behind them. Far right, after the saplings have been steamed, Roy and his son, Merle, bend the hickory saplings into a jig where they will dry overnight. At bottom, a handwritten "Smile — God Loves You" sign, a testament to the Yoders' outlook on life, is tacked on the wall of the family workshop.

Bob Reaume

farrier

"I've always had a horse bug," said 68-year-old Bob Reaume (REE-um), who started shoeing horses on the family farm in the early '40s.

"Around the Second World War, things started to get pretty well mechanized, and the draft horse got phased out. Horse numbers started declining really fast. I started nailing shoes on my horses then because all the shoers were gone.

"There was one still around, but his son got a draft deferment so he could shoe the workhorses and he wouldn't touch the light ones. So I used the braille method and taught myself how to do it. I got really intrigued."

Reaume took his interest to Michigan State University for a degree in animal husbandry but detoured for a while to study horseshoeing in the MSU program that taught practical things, such as animal breeding and crop science, during the winters so farmers could attend.

"It was the only school for horseshoeing in the United States," said Reaume. With the skills he learned there, he worked the horseshoeing circuit in central Michigan in the 1950s and '60s.

"It was about this time that the saddle horses started to come back. And all of a sudden, there was a big demand for horseshoers, carriage makers and harness makers — for all those trades that had disappeared."

He opened the Wolverine Farrier School in 1972 to teach others his blacksmithing art.

"The population of horses has leveled off now," said Reaume. "It's even declined, but the quality of our work has risen."

Bob Reaume's schoolhouse, at left, has a smokestack for each of the forges where students learn to make horseshoes. Above, the teacher is shown inside the school in 1987. "It takes a lot of work to be certified with the American Farrier Association," he says. "Years ago, anybody who could nail a shoe on a horse could learn some of the basics and go out and buy ready-made shoes and get all the work they wanted. But nowadays, it's a different story. The standards have risen. A shoeing school is just a start. You gotta go out and keep improving your skills." Nearly 600 students from around the world have come to stay at Reaume's 96-acre farm near Cohoctah in Livingston County and learn from him.

Machine-made blank horseshoes take only a few minutes to be fitted to a horse, but it takes a lot of skill and a fair amount of pounding to forge the custom-made shoes Reaume's students learn to make at the Wolverine Farrier School. At far right, one of Reaume's students shapes a shoe on an anvil in 1987; below, the tools of the farrier's trade hanging in Bob Reaume's classroom and workshop. Reaume still gets a kick out of shoeing horses. "I do it to get the biggest charge," says the farrier. His skills were in greatest demand beginning in the early 1950s, when the horse population of the United States jumped from a low of three million to over 12 million. It has leveled off over the last decade or so, Reaume says. "When we started, I'd hold three 16-week classes a year. Now I only hold one class in the wintertime." Reaume, who grew up in Dearborn, always has a few horses on his Livingston County farm.

Above, Reaume's students work at the forges inside the school. They start with steel bars and heat them in the small furnaces until they are hot enough to be flattened and shaped into custom shoes for a perfect fit on individual horses' hooves. "Every time you make a set of shoes you try to make 'em a little faster and a little better," says the teacher. "The standards for the horses have gone so high I don't believe it. All this skill has accumulated over the years. If I did this for 110 years I'd still be way behind," Reaume says. Mike Janin, one of the students at Wolverine Farrier School in 1987, says Reaume "has the patience of a saint."

The cat doesn't bother Edmund Whitepigeon as he works on a basket outside the home of his son, Steven Pigeon, in 1988. Above, Whitepigeon teaches his daughter-in-law, Kathy Pigeon, how to make the black ash baskets. He makes them in distinctive styles – a twill weave with a diamond design, and a geometric arrow design, both in rainbow colors. Whitepigeon, a retired construction worker, lives with his wife, Jennie, near Dorr in Allegan County. The town of White Pigeon in St. Joseph County was named after his great-great-grandfather, Wahbememe (WAH-ba-meme), which means White Pigeon in the Ojibwa language.

Edmund Whitepigeon Julia Wesaw

black ash basket makers

The ancestors of today's multiethnic family of Michigan arrived almost a thousand years ago. The Ottawa and Ojibwa settled up north and the Potawatomi in the Lower Peninsula.

With longer summers and better soils to work with, the Potawatomi took to an agricultural lifestyle vastly different from the foraging culture of their northern kin.

Stored harvests and abundant wildlife helped the Potawatomi build villages and devote time to social awareness and political dealings with neighboring tribes. New tools were introduced, free time was found and new ideas came into the band. Even with the influx of the new, the southernmost of Michigan's woodland tribes held on to some of the old arts and passed them down to the children.

Julia Wesaw of Hartford learned the art of black ash basket making from her grandmother. Edmund Whitepigeon of Dorr learned from his father. Julia Wesaw passed the tradition on to her children before she died at age 79 in 1992. At age 75, Edmund Whitepigeon is still teaching the art to his grandchildren, Little Bear and Thunder Lady.

Julia Wesaw shows off two of her favorite baskets. Below left is a market basket with sturdy handles and, above, a small basket with lid.

Above, Julia Wesaw works on her baskets in the enclosed porch of her home in Van Buren County in 1988. Julia would frequently participate in festivals and basket-making expositions around Michigan. Besides her art, her legacy is the encouragement she gave to young people to learn their traditions, from black ash basket making to beadwork to the construction of birchbark canoes.

Above, Eli Thomas at the door of his home in Mt. Pleasant in 1988. At right, he wears an elaborate headdress.

Eli Thomas
Don Stevens

tribal elders

There are more stories to tell about Michigan's first residents than Longfellow's "The Song of Hiawatha." In fact, Hiawatha was a folk legend among the Iroquois, who were mortal enemies of Michigan's woodland tribes, the Ottawa, Ojibwa and Potawatomi.

Don Stevens, also called Red Arrow, and Eli Thomas, known as Little Elk, *Anishnabe* elders, have spent their lives telling the stories of their people to all who wish to listen.

Stevens, who lives in Blanchard, and Thomas, who made his home in Mt. Pleasant, have traveled across North America, sharing the songs and dances of their ancestors and telling the Indian folk legends that form the basis of their values and beliefs.

Many members of Stevens' family — cousins and all — have made their living for years re-creating and selling unusual tools and crafts of the Ojibwa, such as racks used for stretching and drying animal skins.

Thomas was a respected medicine man who oversaw sacred ceremonies, including the naming of the children.

Stevens, 59, and his family continue their work, trying to keep alive the reminders of their traditional ways. Thomas died in 1990 at age 92.

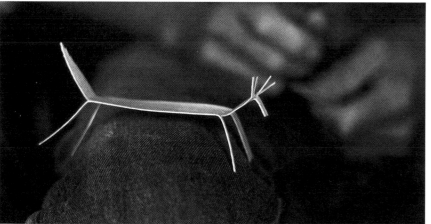

Above, Don Stevens uses a knife on a piece of cattail reed outside his home in Blanchard in 1988. In his work, he uses natural materials to show that his ancestors made good use of what they had available in order to build a life for themselves and their children. At left is a small toy Stevens made in the shape of an animal. Little wooden toys such as this one were made by *Anishnabe* fathers for their children when Michigan was still a vast wilderness. Stevens and many of his relatives make and sell everything from toys to the practical items used by their ancestors.

Sally Thielen

mask maker

"I try to create art," said Sally Thielen (THEEE-len) "with harmony and balance of ancient and contemporary ideas."

The art that Thielen creates blends two cultures. She makes sculptured facial masks of *raku* porcelain, Japanese pottery that dates back to the 16th Century, and decorates them with deer antlers, ermine fur and bird feathers. The result is a modern-looking version of the masks made by American Indians for thousands of years.

"The masks are spiritual," said Thielen, 54, who has Chippewa ancestors. "They are not to be confused with the ceremonial ones. Mine are more of an historical representative of the person, a cultural representation."

She starts by mixing plaster and applying it to her subject's face to make a mold. Straws are placed in the nostrils so the person can breathe for the 10 to 15 minutes it takes the plaster to dry enough to be removed.

When the plaster is completely dry, she rolls a piece of soft porcelain clay flat like a pancake and presses it into the mold. "Now I have a positive of the face," said Thielen. "I bore holes into it for the antlers, cut the eye holes out if I want them to be open, then let it dry."

Masks are baked at 1,600 to 1,800 degrees in an electric kiln in the backyard of her home near Davison. After they have cooled, she applies glaze and puts the masks in a gas-fired kiln for a second firing, till the glaze is like melted butter. The masks then go into a garbage can full of leaves to cool down. "They try to burn, but there's not enough oxygen and they just smolder," said Thielen. "That causes the effect of those beautiful rainbow-like colors that come from *raku*. It also brings out the luster."

Thielen, who has been making the masks since 1978, uses feathers, antlers and other natural materials to decorate them. "What the Creator gives me, in the color of the firing, is what I get. It's what I work with." At left, top to bottom: "Winter Essence," "Hidden Persona" and "Doorwatcher." Above, Thielen and her mask, "Looks Ahead," in the hallway of her home.

Above, Thielen applies plaster to the face of her husband, Bob, in 1989. "This doesn't work too well with beards," she says. "When you pull the plaster off, the beard wants to go with it." At left, Thielen applies glaze to a clay mask before firing it for the second time; at far left, decorated masks are fired in her backyard kiln. "I have this feeling that I'm recording people who are living now for future times, because it will be the exact person, not a painting," she says. All the masks that Thielen makes for display in art galleries or for sale are made from molds of her Indian friends, and she gives them masks made from their faces as a thank-you. At right, from top: an untitled piece, "Tom Deerdancing" and "Southern Traveler," her self-portrait.

Diane Tite

baker

It started 30 years ago for Diane Tite of Marine City.

"We went to the state fair and were looking at the baking contest entries when my husband said, 'You can bake just as good as they do.' So I tried it and won the next year."

Every year since then, Tite, 55, has been entering cinnamon rolls, bacon-chive buns, dinner rolls, coffee cakes and other kitchen goodies, mostly in the yeast breads category of the baking contest at the Michigan State Fair. She has won more than a few first prizes.

In 1992, she went home with six first-place ribbons out of her 10 entries. She says lots of practice and a good teacher are her secrets.

"I learned this as a little kid," said Tite, whose mom, Kathleen Smith, still shows her how to do things "the right way."

"She showed me how to work with the yeast, how it feels," said Tite. "She taught me things you could never learn in a book. Heck, she still gives me pointers whenever we're in the kitchen together."

The family secrets are being passed on to the next generation. Tite's three sons and three daughters all learned their way around the kitchen as children.

"When I was a little kid, my friends would always want to come over to our house and play," said son William, who enters his apple pies in state and county fairs. "There were always fresh cookies or pies. Mom always had something she just baked lying around."

"It's fun competing at the fairs," said Diane Tite, who has been a finalist in the Pillsbury Bake-Off competition, "and a bit strange. Most of my competitors are men."

Above, Diane Tite and her son William at work in her kitchen in Marine City in 1993. On the production line are Diane's cinnamon rolls and William's apple pie. William, 35, has been entering cooking and baking contests since he was a child. At the 1993 state fair, William's apple pie didn't win, but his cheese ball made with Spam and toasted almonds won a second prize. His mom won five blue ribbons — for her dinner rolls, bacon-chive buns, English muffins, pineapple jam and strawberry jam. Diane Tite gives her mom, Kathleen Smith, much of the credit, and, at right, a hug.

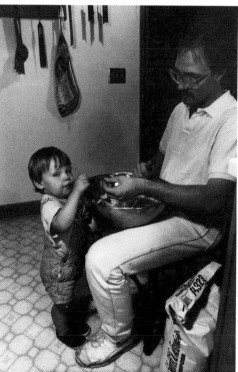

In her kitchen, Diane Tite displays freshly made cinnamon rolls, ready to be baked. "Don't put in too much sugar and don't put in too little cinnamon," she advises. At right, above, some of the first-place ribbons she has won. William Tite's son, Stuart, 2, helps himself to some of his dad's apple slices in grandma's kitchen. It's a little early for him to be manning the mixing bowls, but Diane Tite wouldn't be surprised if Stuart becomes part of the next generation of family bakers. "He certainly has the appetite for it," she says, laughing.

Doctor Ross

blues player

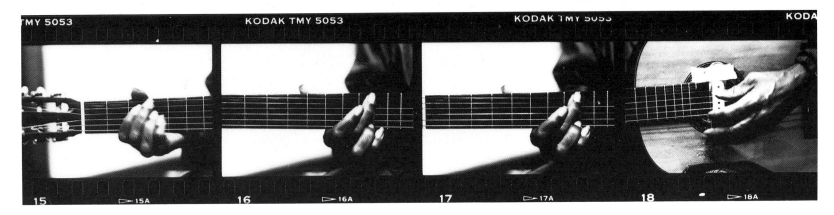

When Isaiah Ross came home to the States on furlough during World War II, his friends told him, "We been sick since you been gone, now we gonna call you 'Doctor.'"

Born in Tunica, Mississippi, Isaiah Ross started playing music when he was 6. He would take his father's harmonicas off the mantel and sneak in some playing while his father was at work. He'd tell his friends, "Don't tell Papa."

One day, his father overheard him playing and said: "God sends talent. You hit some keys I never heard before."

After that, he was allowed to play at parties and wherever he wanted, as long as he was home by 8 p.m. On a clear night, the music could be heard for miles. "I can remember walking down the old road and playing after dark," Ross said. "You could see the folks two miles away turn their lights on."

The nickname he picked up during the service stuck. Dr. Ross recorded songs and drew attention in the late '40s and early '50s with his Mississippi Delta-style blues. One of the stories he liked to tell was about meeting Elvis Presley when Presley was trying to bum $20 from Ross' recording boss. A fallout with the recording company led Ross to Flint and a job at General Motors.

During his years at GM, he played around the country at blues concerts and festivals and traveled periodically to Europe for concert tours. After nearly 40 years on the job, he was planning to retire from GM in late 1993 and devote more time to his music. But on May 28, at 67, Dr. Ross had a heart attack at the Chevrolet plant and died.

Above, in 1987, Dr. Ross plays the blues on his guitar. In his words, "Blues is truth. If it didn't happen to you, it happened to someone else." How did the doctor define the blues? "If you love a woman, and you do everything you can for her, and maybe she shacks up with another guy - that ain't nothing but the blues."

Dr. Ross holds some of the tools of the blues trade. Above, he spreads the "boogie disease," the doctor's description of his music. The words to one of his early songs, "Boogie Disease," say it all: "gonna boogie for the doctor/gonna boogie for the nurse/gonna keep on boogiein' till they throw me in the hearse … "

DOCTOR ROSS
1925-1993

Above, Eva Wang concentrates on a cutout in her workshop. She makes a variety of designs, as the collage of cutouts on her worktable shows. At right, it takes patience and practice to make clean, steady cuts without tearing the paper. Wang prefers to work with only one layer of paper at a time. Below, butterflies alight in her hand.

Eva Wang

paper cutter

The rice paper cutouts are sometimes called window flowers.

In ancient China, they were used to add color and for decoration on rice paper windows that were made translucent with tung oil. The delicate, detailed cutouts are still used during festive occasions and as good luck charms.

"It is my family's tradition," said 77-year-old Eva Wang. "We'd cut them out and use them to decorate gifts."

As many as 20 cutouts can be made at the same time, depending on the thickness of the paper. Designs are drawn on one piece of thin paper and placed over layers of even thinner rice paper. The artist holds the cutting tool as if it were a pen or pencil and creates the design. *Chien chih,* or cut paper, has been found in tombs dating to the Sixth Century.

It is still a tradition to decorate windows for the celebration of the Chinese lunar New Year, which occurs in January or February.

"The work is art symbolism," said Chen-Oi Hsieh, director of the Chinese-American Educational and Cultural Center of Michigan in Ann Arbor. "They were used as kitchen gods, bookmarks and symbols of good luck, prosperity and fertility. In about a year, the old paper windows and cutouts would fade and be replaced, but the old window frames were saved."

Wang learned the art from her mother as she was growing up in Hunan province. "I only make them now for the very special occasions," said Wang, who has lived in East Lansing since 1980. "My granddaughter just got married, so the next one I make will be for my first great-grandchild."

Helene Lewis

doll maker

"I always liked antique dolls," said Helene Lewis, "and I knew I could never afford one of them, so I learned how to make my own."

In 1985, Lewis, 59, began taking classes to learn about porcelain dolls and soon started making antique-style dolls, the kind her mother played with as a child.

Porcelain, fine-grained, nonporous china of the type used to make delicate ceramic ware, is poured into a clay mold to form the head, and sometimes the arms and hands of the dolls. After setting for 20 minutes to a half hour, the pieces are removed and allowed to cure overnight. Then Lewis lightly sands and cleans the doll parts until they are "just the way I want them."

Once cleaned, the doll parts are kiln-fired to harden them, and the painting begins. If a little color in the cheeks is desired, it is painted on and the pieces are kiln-fired again to set the color. Then the eyelashes are painted on and the head is re-fired. Then the lips are colored in and the pieces are fired again. Some pieces may be fired up to 10 times to achieve the desired effect.

When a doll's head has been painted, the eyes are set in and the wig is attached. Then comes the fun part — dressing the doll up. "I go through old fashion magazines, family pictures, anything to get an idea," said Lewis, who makes the dolls in a small shop behind the family horse barn just outside Dryden in Lapeer County.

"The outfit on the doll I made this year that just won the best of show award at the Michigan State Fair," she said in 1993, "was a copy of my father's christening gown."

Above, in 1993, Helene Lewis shows off Lady Grace, the doll she made that won best of show at the 1992 Michigan State Fair. "This is just a fun hobby for me. I never sell them," says Lewis. "After you make them, you kind of hate to part with them. I talk to them a bit. It's kind of like creating little people. They become real hard to part with." At right, she holds the rounded glass eyes that she uses to give a doll's face a realistic look. Lewis collects jewelry and old clothes at flea markets, garage sales, or "wherever I can find them," and uses them to dress up her dolls. "I really love the whole process," she says.

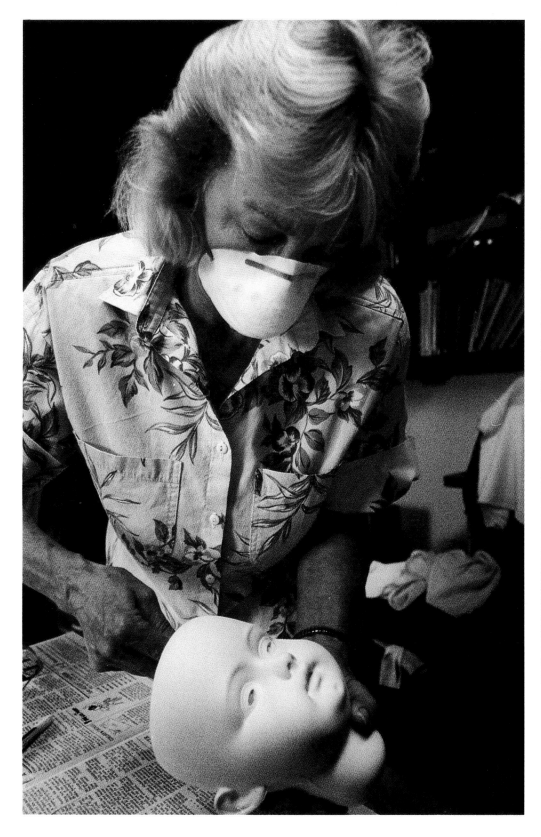

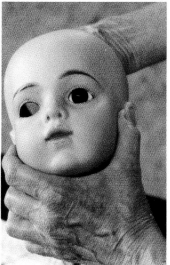

Clockwise, from near left: Lewis inserts the eyes into a doll's head, then paints on eyebrows, lashes and lips. She cleans a newly molded head while wearing a surgical mask as protection from the fine dust that can be hazardous if inhaled. Lewis has been teaching her 10-year-old granddaughter, Margaux Germonprez, how to make dolls. Margaux has learned her lessons so well that she won the blue ribbon for doll making in the Michigan State Fair youth division in 1992. Above, Margaux adjusts a bonnet on the doll that won her first place.

Poletown Cadillac plant
Wayne County

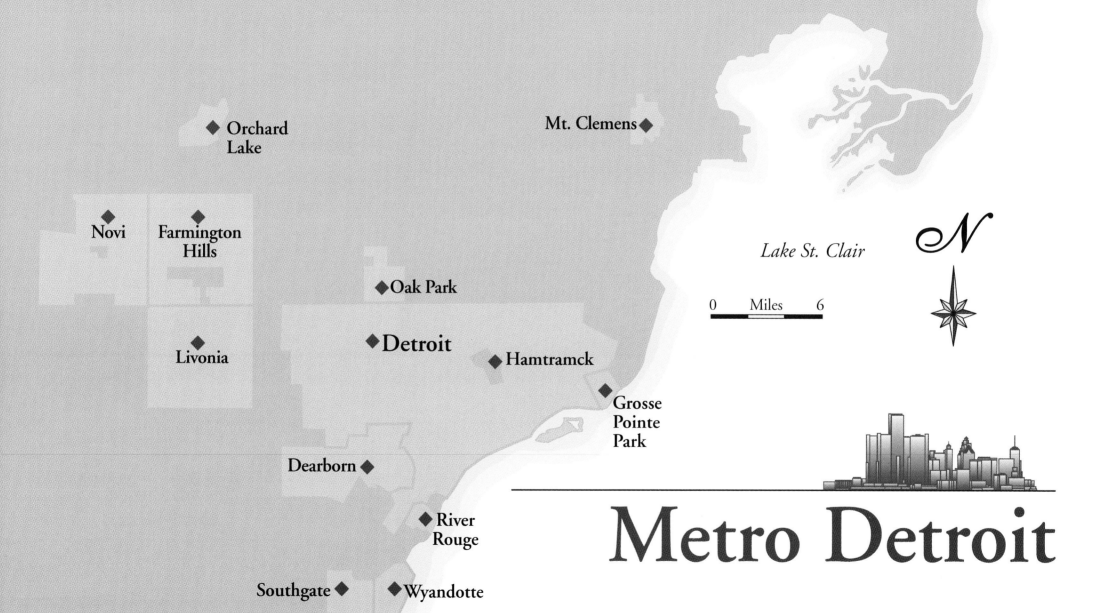

Orchard
Lake

Mt. Clemens

Novi Farmington
Hills

Lake St. Clair

Oak Park

0   Miles   6

Detroit

Livonia

Hamtramck

Grosse
Pointe
Park

Dearborn

River
Rouge

Southgate Wyandotte

Metro Detroit

Samiha Abusalah
Amneh Baraka

embroiderers

Samiha Abusalah (sa-ME-ha AH-boo-sah-lah) wanted a *thobe,* the floor-length ornate dress worn by women from the Middle East and knew she could never afford one.

"Everybody had one and I didn't," said Abusalah. "Amneh Baraka (EM-na BEAR-a-gah) was living upstairs and she was making them for a living and I became interested," said Abusalah, whose parents moved to the United States from Palestine when she was 14 years old. "I really wanted to see what she was doing.

"I was just married and I couldn't come up with three or four hundred dollars for a dress, so I went to Amneh and learned how to make one," said Abusalah, 35, who lives in the Moslem community of Arab Americans in southeast Dearborn. "It took me a year, but I was able to make my first dress."

Palestinian women do most of their own embroidery, said Abusalah. The work is done in sections called stripes. "A lot of women will do their own stripes and then give them to Amneh to attach them together. That's the hard part," Abusalah said.

Thobes are usually made in five parts — the front, back, two sleeves and bodice. "They are all attached by hand, not machine," said Abusalah, "and Amneh is one of the few who know how to do it."

Abusalah has made five of the traditional Palestinian dresses since taking lessons from Amneh and has gone on to teach embroidery.

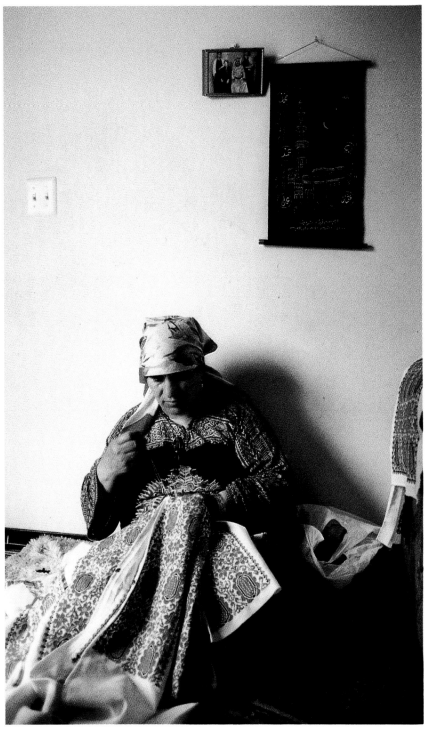

At left, Amneh Baraka sews together embroidered stripes to make a *thobe* in her home in 1990. The ankle-length dress is sewn entirely by hand. Five stripes that will form a dress are embroidered in colorful and traditional patterns, such as the stripe above. Below, Samiha Abusalah, in the middle, helps her friends, Helen Atwell, left, and Mary Shihadeh, right, with their embroidery on the front porch of her home in 1990. "If my children want to learn, I will teach them," says Samiha, who has three daughters and two sons. "But it will be totally up to them."

Homayed family

bakers

It's a typical neighborhood operation where you stop in for a loaf of bread and a quart of milk or maybe a can of Homos Tehini, a freshly baked piece of Zahtar bread and some Halawa sesame dessert with a few Kaak cookies.

The Arabian Village Bakery in southeast Dearborn is part of the biggest Arab community this side of the Atlantic Ocean. The bakery has been owned by Susie Homayed (ho-MAY-yed) and her husband, Saleh (SAL-eh), since 1973.

"My grandfather brought my family over here," said Susie, who is Lebanese. "He moved here in the 1920s and thought it was a good place to bring up kids. So my parents came over in 1947, just before I was born."

Susie, 45, and Saleh, 55, who is from Lebanon, were married in 1964. She worked for National Bank of Detroit in downtown Detroit while Saleh was working for Ford Motor Co. at the sprawling Rouge complex that can be seen from all the streets in Dearborn's Muslim community.

"Saleh got hurt in '73 and couldn't work for Ford's anymore," said Homayed, "so we had to come up with something else."

What they came up with was the bakery. "We started out doing a little baking," said Susie Homayed, "just baking bread, along with meat and cheese pies.

"Then we started carrying milk, then rice and olive oil, a little of this and a little of that. You gotta do what you gotta do, and we did."

Susie and Saleh Homayed's Arabian Village Bakery is no ordinary corner store. At right, in 1989, Susie Homayed holds a tray of baked goods with aromas that entice. On the tray are *fatayeh*, or meat pies, and fried kibbe pies made without fat and stuffed with meat and pine nuts. Besides selling baked goods and groceries, the shop always has something delicious cooking for the customers.

Above, Saleh Homayed is making *shawarma*, gyro-style lamb and beef that will be sliced for sandwiches. Arabic and English are spoken in equal proportions in the store, where it's not unusual to see customers walk out with Tootsie Roll Pops in their pockets and a 50-pound bag of bulgur wheat over their shoulders. The Homayeds run the store with full-time help from their oldest son, Ali, 25, and part-time help from their seven other children.

Rev. Czeslaw Krysa

egg writer

In the United States, they're known as Easter eggs. In Poland, they've been calling them *pisanki* (pea-SAHN-key) for more than a thousand years.

Pisanki, "signed" or "written" Easter eggs, have been found in homes in the central Slavic region of Europe since the 10th Century.

The people of several Eastern European nations claim *pisanki* as their creation. "We don't exactly know where they started decorating the eggs for Easter," said the Rev. Czeslaw M. Krysa (CHESS-swaff CHRIS-ah), a professor of liturgical studies at SS. Cyril and Methodius Seminary in Orchard Lake. "The oldest archaeological evidence points to Poland."

Krysa, 39, starting decorating eggs 25 years ago in his hometown of Niagara Falls, New York. "My father, Stanislaw, came from the part of Poland where they did *pisanki*, and I learned the basics from him.

"As I grew up, I had to search for designs," Krysa said. "In 1977, I made a trip to Poland to visit my great-aunt, Stanislawa Dudzinska-Paul. We called her Ciocia Paulka — Aunt Paula. She was the master *pisanki* writer in the family, and I saw the way she signed the eggs of spring. That's where I really learned the art. I sketched some designs and started my first formal research into *pisanki*."

Krysa's collection totals more than 900 *pisanki*, 650 made by him. "I still make some one-color eggs and eat them for Easter, but I hold on to all the *pisanki*."

Rev. Czeslaw Krysa writes on an egg in molten black wax with a copper stylus attached to a stick. When the egg is immersed in dye, the shell retains its previous color wherever the wax has been applied. The pattern is then added to, the egg immersed in another dye, and so on. As the heat from a candle gently melts off the wax, above, the colors reappear and form the design. At far right, some of the dye has been scratched off to show a scene on a finished egg.

At left, Krysa works on *pisanki* just before Easter in 1991. Jars of dye, lots of wax, a good supply of eggs and skill are needed. It is up to the individual artist whether or not to blow out the egg contents through a pinhole after the *pisanki* designs are completed. Since 1984, Krysa has visited more than 50 museums in Poland to learn about traditional designs, such as those above. In 1993, he received an arts grant to teach egg writing to an apprentice. "It is a fascinating form of art. It's so different. It's the oldest form of egg decorating," Krysa says. He keeps all his *pisanki* now, but when he was a child, "we did them for the Easter basket and we'd eat them right away."

Sudha Chandrasekhar

dancer

"My mom was my very first teacher. She was my most important guru," said Sudha Chandrasekhar (SUE-dah CHAN-dra-shaker). "She knew I had this dance in me."

The dance is Bharata Natyam (bah-REHT-ah not-TIEM). According to Hindu teachings, Natarajah, the lord of dancing, presented it as a gift to Bharata, a Hindu sage, around 200 B.C.

"It's both art and religion," said Chandrasekhar, 53, of Oak Park. "And it's too precious to let disappear."

She started dancing when she was 3 years old in Bombay, India. "While I was going to school, I learned the Mani Puri dance of northeast India and Katha Kali, a dance drama from southern India.

"My mother saw the interest I developed, she saw the passion, the obsession I had for dance, and she waited until the best teachers were available. Kuppiah Pillai, my dance guru, moved to Bombay from the south of India and, with other members of his family, shared with me the knowledge of Bharata Natyam."

In 1956, Chandrasekhar started dancing professionally in India and gained international fame with more than 2,000 performances. She began teaching Bharata Natyam at age 18. When she moved to the United States in 1978, the teaching took over.

"I feel the children need direction, and the art needs to be kept alive. As well as dance, I try to teach the children the traditional values and customs, to appreciate where they came from and what they have. I try to explain to them how we can still find use for age-old values in today's world."

Sudha Chandrasekhar in her Bharata Natyam dance costume, left, and in everyday dress, above. The jewelry is worn as an adornment to bring out the beauty of the dance. Chandrasekhar's two hair ornaments represent the sun and the moon. The center of the hair is parted and covered with a third adornment that brings out the contour of the face. Large necklaces are worn to camouflage the heavy breathing that comes with the dancing. The spot in the center of the forehead is the *pottu*, marking the place where knowledge is revealed to us as sacred. It's the third eye that humans are believed to possess, the eye that opens only when a person concentrates.

Sudha Chandrasekhar's 16-year-old daughter, Anandini (ah-nun-DIN-knee), or "the joyous one," uses her eyes and her hands to help convey the meaning behind the dance. Her hands move from the center of her face to the sides to accentuate her eyes and enhance the expression.

Above, Monica Bhatt, 14, paints the hand of Shivani Kaul, 17, before Sudha Chandrasekhar's class at the Bharatiya Temple in Troy one Saturday in 1993. Chandrasekhar's daughter Anjali, 18, is in the background. Designs, or *alta,* are painted on the hands to draw attention to the movements and hand gestures, called *mudras,* which tell the stories. At right, Chandrasekhar adjusts a choker on her daughter Vidya, 24, before practice begins at home. Vidya has been taking lessons from her mother since she learned how to walk. Generally, women dancers represent Saraswathi, the Hindu goddess of art and learning. By adorning themselves, they are honoring the goddess.

"I'm doing the role of the mother figure and Vidya is the daughter," says Chandrasekhar, at right, above. The mother is trying to feed her daughter a morsel of food and the daughter says, "No, not now." It is from one of the stories told in Bharata Natyam. In India, says Chandrasekhar, "I lived in a Brahman community and led a very sheltered life. Young women were not allowed to go out by themselves. We always had escorts." When Chandrasekhar came to the United States as a grown woman, one of her goals was to teach dancing to young women and at the same time, perpetuate a respect for the traditional values she grew up with.

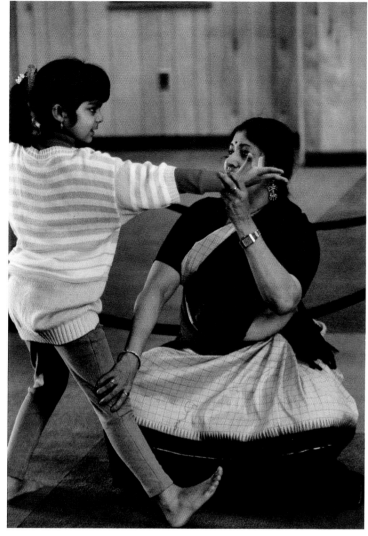

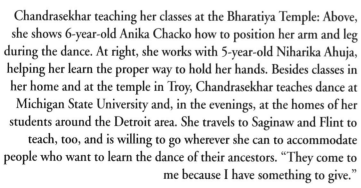

Chandrasekhar teaching her classes at the Bharatiya Temple: Above, she shows 6-year-old Anika Chacko how to position her arm and leg during the dance. At right, she works with 5-year-old Niharika Ahuja, helping her learn the proper way to hold her hands. Besides classes in her home and at the temple in Troy, Chandrasekhar teaches dance at Michigan State University and, in the evenings, at the homes of her students around the Detroit area. She travels to Saginaw and Flint to teach, too, and is willing to go wherever she can to accommodate people who want to learn the dance of their ancestors. "They come to me because I have something to give."

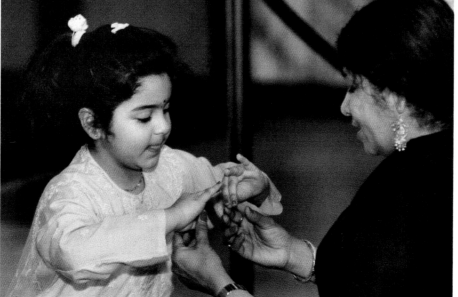

Above, Shubha Chakraborty watches her teacher, Sudha Chandrasekhar, during Shubha's first class at the temple. "The main purpose of the dancer, the devotee," says Chandrasekhar, "is to remind the onlookers about the supreme greatness of God and his existence. And to build in them a feeling of devotion, hope and faith. I want to teach this to my students, and their job is to spread it to the world."

Sonnie Perez

pinata maker

As Sonia Marie Perez starts work on a new pinata (pin-YAH-ta), she starts telling its history.

"In every little town in Mexico, the people would bring their animals, their fruit, their crops to the village plaza to be blessed on Harvest Day," said Perez, who lives in Livonia.

"The villagers would decorate the pottery bowls they carried parts of their harvest in. As time went on, it started to become a contest. The prettiest bowl would be hung from a tree in the plaza and blindfolded children would take turns swinging at it with a stick, trying to break it open and capture the fruit, candy, nuts and little toys that were hidden inside."

Harvest Day celebrations were carried over to Christmas, then birthdays and weddings.

"You know, the odd thing is, my mother never made them," said Perez, a 75-year old great-grandmother.

Her family settled in Detroit in the '20s, and Perez was raised in the Mexican-American community on the city's southwest side.

"My family life was totally Mexican," said Perez, nicknamed "Sonnie" by her friends. "All our food was Mexican, we never spoke English in the house, and my father traveled the migrant work camps all over the United States.

"When my brother returned from World War II," said Perez, "he helped form the American Legion Mexican-American Post 505 in Detroit. I joined the auxiliary in 1945 and when I was made entertainment chairman in '47, I really got interested in doing something ethnic."

Sonnie Perez, left, with two of her pinatas, a lion and Fernando the Matador, at her home in 1989. Below, a finished member of Perez's papier-mache mariachi band and an unfinished accompanist. Strips of newspaper are dipped into a water-and-flour mixture and placed over balloons to form the pinatas. Perez started making papier-mache pinatas after an American Legion post picnic when one of the members raised a pinata from Mexico. Perez worried that the children would cut themselves on the pot shards as they broke it open and scrambled for the candy. "So, I tried to make one out of papier-mache so the children wouldn't get hurt, and it worked."

Above, Perez applies a mouth to a new member of her orchestra. Once the papier-mache newspaper strips have dried, the figures are painted and accessories added. Perez makes hats and musical instruments and other additions out of papier-mache or cardboard. At right, Perez folds strips of brightly colored paper that will be cut and glued onto the lion.

Above, eyes are glued onto Perez's mariachi musician at the Perez pinata workshop, her kitchen table.

From Aztec days through revolutionary times, Perez's papier-mache dolls trace the history of Mexico. From left, the last two rulers of the Aztec empire, Cuauhtemoc and Montezuma. In the middle, the mariachi pinata. Next is Pancho Villa, the famous guerrilla leader. At far right is a farmer, with sword and bandolier, representing citizens who fought for independence from Spain. In front, an Aztec weaver and loom.

Howard Armstrong

musician

Howard Armstrong, 84, was born in Dayton, Tennessee, "into a music family. It's in my genes."

Armstrong's older brother and three older sisters formed a band and performed "at funerals, weddings, parties, proms, just about everything and anything, black and white. Sometimes they would bring home some food, maybe chickens."

The group broke up as his sisters married and moved away. "That's when I was learning how to play the fiddle my father made me and the mandolin. After I learned, I taught my four younger brothers and we had another family band for a few more years." Armstrong moved to Knoxville when he was 15 and started to learn from the black street musicians.

Armstrong and three of his new friends formed the Four Keys and "played all over the place" before breaking up in the mid-'30s. He got married and headed back to Tennessee to work the factories and paint signs.

Near the end of World War II, Armstrong settled in Detroit. "I was playing my music a little, but painting a lot. I painted signs on trucks, on windows, did murals, painted churches. I painted anything. That's how I fed those little crumb snatchers," he said with a grin, referring to his four sons. Now, Armstrong plays with his son Rapp and travels the country teaching and playing a type of music that has been around for 200 years.

Howard Armstrong's living room wall, shown below in 1990, is decorated with awards he has received and tikis that he makes and sells. "They bring good luck. The more I sell, the luckier I am," says the man born on the day William Howard Taft was inaugurated. "He's the reason I got my name." Music was a family tradition. "My father made me my first violin. I went down the alley looking for a wooden goods box. He cut it out and varnished it and I learned to play it." Armstrong's bluesy jazz landed him the nickname "Louie Bluie" when a young woman told him, "I know your name is Armstrong, but you're not Louie Armstrong. You're just plain old Louie Bluie." In the early '70s Armstrong teamed up with two musician friends from the '30s and his son Tommy. "I bet we played every country in South America." Now he tours with another son. "As long as somebody is interested, I will perform."

Michigan

A grand magnificent state, a great lake as a coastal;

Since its founding all its fields have flourished;

Its auto industry keeps America moving and enjoys fame in distant lands;

Its factories and farms, scientists and scholars stand together in the forefront;

The Tigers and the Lions prowl for pennants;

Its people have hearts of pure gold;

Its government coffers are heaped full;

The scenic beauty of its four seasons is a treasure all can afford;

Its prospects dazzle.

By Po-Ling Cheng

Po-Ling Cheng and his granddaughter Christina, 8, hold a copy of his poem "Michigan." In Chinese calligraphy, he speaks of his love for his adopted home.

Po-Ling Cheng

calligrapher

"I can do this, but I'm just a student," said 84-year-old Po-Ling Cheng of Farmington Hills. "My grandfather was an expert."

Cheng uses brushes to create the complex, picture-like symbols that make up traditional Chinese calligraphy. Pictographs were first used for Chinese writing around 1400 B.C. Similar to Egyptian hieroglyphs, pictographs are simple images used to express ideas. Traces of the original styles are still seen in today's writing, which has evolved through six stages into thousands of characters representing various concepts.

Calligraphy couplets are the greeting cards of China. These are small poems or quoted verse and are signs of friendship, best wishes, condolences and other expressions of feelings.

Cheng has been developing his skill in the calligraphy of his native language for nearly three-quarters of a century. He was born on mainland China and lived there until 1949, when he moved to Taiwan. After many years as a government worker, Cheng retired and moved to the United States in 1983, where his children had made their home.

"Back when my father went to school," said Cheng's son, Peter, "the students learned to write with the brush pen. That was the writing style of the times."

"All the students were learning some of the writing in school," Po-Ling Cheng said, "but my father and grandfather taught me at home. It's so interesting and there is so much to learn." Cheng teaches the traditional style to those "willing to learn."

"I'm teaching my youngest granddaughter, Christina, how to write with the brush pen," said Cheng. "And she's teaching me how to write in English. Only," he added with a smile, "she says I'm not doing too good."

At left, Cheng works on a greeting from Leo Ho, a government representative from Taiwan, to Michigan's U.S. Sen. Carl Levin in 1991, congratulating him for excellence in Washington. Above, the brushes used in calligraphy are the same as those used in fine art painting. Cheng is modest about his skill and says that his grandfather, his first calligraphy teacher, was the expert. Peter Cheng has a son's respect for his father's work: "If he was born a thousand years ago he would have been a famous calligrapher, but today, people don't pay attention to his art."

Lower right, children watch Cheng at work at the Chinese-American Educational and Cultural Center in Ann Arbor. "I have been studying this since I was 10 years old," says Cheng. "But even if I live to be 200, I don't think I'll learn it all." Although Cheng moved to the United States late in life, he enjoys Western ways and has even adopted an English first name, Winston, because he liked the way Winston Churchill held his cigars. At near right, Cheng writes good-luck characters to make a greeting for a friend. Far right, Cheng holds a calligrapher's bible, a Chinese dictionary.

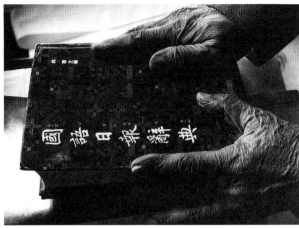

Belgian bowlers

cheese bowlers
floor bowlers

They say it started many years ago, but nobody knows when or where. Legend has it that a wheel of cheese fell off a wagon going uphill on its way to market in Flanders, and those who watched it roll downhill in the hard-packed, clay wagon wheel rut came up with a great idea. Cheese bowling.

Cheese bowling? Yes, cheese bowling, also referred to as feather bowling. On a slow sales day, buyers and sellers at the Old World markets would pass the time by seeing who could roll waxed pieces of Gouda or Holland cheese directly at a pigeon feather, stuck firmly in a wagon rut on a country road. A pleasant way to pass the day when business stunk.

"We use pigeon feathers because they bend when the ball lands on top of them," said Roger Ghesquiere, a 20th-Century bowler from Michigan. "A pigeon feather will bounce right back up."

Ghesquiere, 65, (GUESS-choir), is president of the Cadieux Bowling Club. He remembers when his father helped build a cheese bowling alley at the Cadieux Cafe on Detroit's east side in 1933.

Down the street in the old Belgian neighborhood sits the Guilford Bar. That's where the Belgian bowlers gather on Saturday night for floor bowling, a game that uses a flatter, sliced-in-half version of the cheese bowling ball. Players crouch and roll the thick disc in a circle, trying to get it to stop in the center. It's a tricky maneuver that calls for good knees — and a lot of patience.

Above is a game of cheese bowling at the Cadieux Cafe in Detroit in 1989. Thursday is bowling night at the cafe, a Belgian sanctuary for bicycle riders, pigeon racers and feather bowlers, where the owners maintain two steeply banked, 72-foot-long, indoor dirt alleys. Although wood has taken the place of cheese, the bowlers still use a pigeon feather as the target. Cheese bowling is done with two teams of three players each. One team uses green balls and the other, red ones. Each player bowls two balls. In every game, only the team that is closest to the feather scores points, one for every ball it gets closer to the feather than the other side. The most points a team can score is six per game, and the first team to reach 10 points wins. It sounds easy, but it isn't. Near right, members of the Saturday night floor bowling club at Guilford Bar and, far right, a bowler holds the flat, disc-shaped ball used in floor bowling.

Edward Baganz

Great Lakes captain

If you ask Ed Baganz a question, he'll answer with another. "That's a long story — you sure you got time?"

Baganz, 93, isn't exaggerating. He tells long stories. But then, he's had a long and eventful life. Capt. Edward C. Baganz, who was skipper of 12 commercial freighters, loves to tell tales of the 51 years he spent sailing more than 2-1/2 million miles on the Great Lakes.

His career started when he was shanghaied on a warm summer day in 1915. "I had a couple of hours for lunch, and I strolled around downtown, admiring the horses — there weren't many cars back then — and I strolled to the river and noticed the Owana, a side-wheeler, a little passenger boat, stopped there at the foot of Woodward.

"A gangplank went down and a brass-button guy came off and says, 'the captain wants to see you.' Of course I didn't know no captain, but I was anxious to get aboard. Looking for excitement, I went aboard and asked where to find the captain, and a cook hands me an apron and says, 'Glad you're gonna help out.' By the time I figured out what was going on, they had pulled away from shore."

Baganz's overnight trip to Port Huron and back launched a lifetime of sailing the inland seas. He settled in with the Pittsburgh Steamship Co., starting as a wheelsman on the whaleback ore carrier John Ericson.

For the next 49 years, Baganz worked his way up the ships' ladders, finally becoming master, or captain, of the Zenith City in 1940. He retired in 1966.

"It wasn't exactly like I expected. I really had to go to work. But I'd do it all again."

Captain Ed Baganz in his Grosse Pointe Park home in 1990 with some of his mementos. He was one of only four commodores of the Pittsburgh Steamship Co., which was a subsidiary of U.S. Steel and, at one time, owner of the largest steamship fleet on the Great Lakes. At right, Baganz shows off a souvenir of his career with U.S. Steel. "I spent eight straight months on the water," he says. "My wife and I would have a honeymoon every year." Baganz's wife, Cecilia, died in 1979. Her ashes were committed to the deep in Lake Superior near Silver Bay, Minnesota. "That's what she wanted. She was a swimmer, and she liked the water. I plan to join her when it's time."

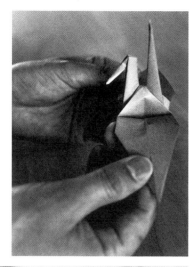

Yoko Sekino

paper folder

Origami (or-uh-GAH-me) is the Japanese art of folding pieces of paper into decorative designs. Six-to-10-inch squares are folded until they look like parrots, cranes, swans, bulls, roosters and many other natural shapes.

Origami is thought to have originated in China, where paper was invented, but it grew into a popular traditional art in Japan. In the past 50 years, complex designs have been added to the 100 or so traditional forms, bringing new challenges to the pastime.

Yoko Sekino (SECK-ee-no), 42, learned origami in school at age 4, as many Japanese children do. She taught her son, Shusuke (SHOOSS-kay), 14, when he was a toddler. But it wasn't until she came to the United States that she realized what she knew was unusual.

The Sekinos moved to Michigan in 1989 when her husband was temporarily assigned to work in the auto industry. Not long after they arrived, Yoko was asked to teach origami to American children.

She spent many hours demonstrating the art to elementary school children and their teachers in Novi. It would take her only a few minutes to show them how to make a small crane, a traditional good-luck piece, or a box-shaped toy that Shusuke and his friends would use to play catch.

The Sekinos returned to Japan in 1993. Back home, near Yokohama, Yoko said she misses the openness of life in Michigan. She said she felt free to reach out to people even though her English wasn't too good. Her Michigan friends thought she spoke beautifully through her art.

Clockwise, from left: Yoko Sekino, in her home in Novi in 1990, shows the variety of shapes that can be made by folding paper. At top left, a crane, which symbolizes long life, is a common origami shape. Above, she shows the piece called "1,000 Cranes," which is made up of many small cranes. The tradition is to give it to someone for good wishes.

Nadeem Dlaikan

flute maker

The music started for Nadeem Dlaikan (na-DEEM dah-LIE-ken) when he was 8 years old and living in his native Lebanon.

"One day I took my brother's flute and tried to play it. He got real mad and hid it and told me not to touch it," said Dlaikan, 52. "So I went down into the valley where the bamboo grows, cut some down, and made a copy of his flute."

Dlaikan, who moved to Michigan in 1971, still is making copies of his brother's shepherd's flute from bamboo that Dlaikan grows in his backyard in Southgate.

"I was visiting my wife's sister in California and saw the bamboo growing all over the place out there and thought, 'Hey, why can't I grow it in Michigan?' " said Dlaikan. "The first year I planted the bulbs, one shoot came up, the second year, two shoots, and more have come up every year since."

He cuts the 18-foot stalks before the frost sets in and stores them in his garage until they dry out. Then he cuts the naturally tapered shoots, hollows them out and glues together pieces of the same length and thickness. After he drills small holes in the bamboo, the flutes are ready to play. The wider and longer the flute, the deeper the sound. Most players carry enough of the bamboo flutes when they perform to allow them to cover the octave range.

"I planted some of the bamboo in my front yard once and people couldn't figure out what it was," said Dlaikan. "Some people thought it was sugar cane. Nobody believed bamboo can grow in Michigan, but it can."

Nadeem Dlaikan tests a new bamboo flute in his garage in 1993. The flutes are a hobby for Dlaikan, who makes his living as a salesman. On the weekends, when he's not making flutes or tending his bamboo, he travels throughout the country, playing traditional Arabic music at parties, weddings and social events. At left, he cuts a piece of bamboo to make the end fit into the next segment of a flute he is making.

Above, after the flute parts have been fitted and glued together, Dlaikan drills holes into the bamboo to complete the instrument. At near right, he looks over his 1993 crop of bamboo. Shepherds began making and playing the flutes as a way to pass the time they spent alone with their flocks.

Dlaikan shows flutes of various sizes which he carries with him when performing to cover the octave range.

Steve Jovanovski

baker

It is a Polish tradition carried on by Macedonian bakers in Hamtramck and Detroit — *Paczki* (POONCH-key) Day.

Paczki are pastries that are filled with fruit jellies or custard and sold before the beginning of Lent, Ash Wednesday. Sweets are traditionally discouraged during Lent, and the last day of caloric indulgence, Fat Tuesday, has come to be known as *Paczki* Day around Detroit.

Steve Jovanovski, 39, has been running the New Polka Bakery in Hamtramck for 13 years. He has seen *Paczki* Day grow into something close to a holiday, the biggest day of the year for his bakery.

"It's slowed down a little in the past few years," said Jovanovski, who lives in Southgate. "The big stores have started carrying *paczki* and taken some of our business away, but we still make more than 2,000 dozen, and we're sold out before Lent."

Steve's father, Mike, came to the United States in 1972 from Macedonia and worked in the auto plants until he was able to purchase the bakery in 1974. Failing eyesight caused him to retire early. Steve, who had joined his family in 1974, took over.

Jovanovski sells Macedonian, Polish and Albanian pastries, pies, cookies and donuts. About 300 loaves of rye, French and pumpernickel bread are made daily for sale at Jovanovski's bakery. Work begins at 5:30 in the morning and doesn't end until after 7 p.m.

"It's a long, hard job," said Jovanovski, "and there aren't many days off. But the people are nice and it's a good living."

Julie Jovanovski, 35, shows off a tray of *paczki* for Fat Tuesday at the New Polka Bakery in 1989. They come filled with raspberry, strawberry, prune, pineapple, apple, blueberry, lemon and custard.

Steve Jovanovski stretches *paczki* dough, below. He and his wife, Julie, have three children — Michael, 3 months; Diane, 6; and Alexander, 13. "I don't know if the children will take over the bakery when they get older," says Steve. "That's still a long way off." At bottom, Mike Jovanovski, Steve's uncle, cuts dough; at right, Steve's dad, Mike, fills *paczki*.

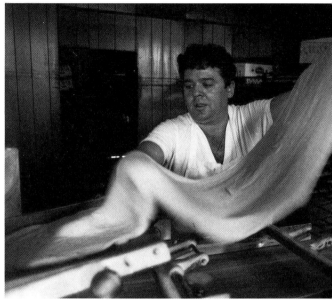

Below, Julie Jolosevich reaches for *paczki* that will go into the deep fryer at the New Polka Bakery in Hamtramck in 1989. Buying dozens of the plump pastries has become a pre-Lenten ritual for many people in the Detroit area. "They're good," says Steve Jovanovski of his *paczki*. Jovanovski's favorite pastry, however, is *tulumba*, a Macedonian honey cake that also is very popular with his customers.

Mabel Damron
George
Williamson

country musicians

They came to Michigan from the battlefield of the Hatfields and the McCoys and brought with them the music that formed the basis of today's country tunes.

Mabel Damron, 70, a coal miner's daughter from Pike County, Kentucky, and her husband, Clark, settled in the Detroit area in the early '40s. George Williamson and his wife, Mary, arrived from the same county of the Bluegrass state in 1949.

"There wasn't nothin' down there but coal mines," said George Williamson, 66, who now lives in Wyandotte. "So I came up here and worked for GM, then Packard, who I helped run out of business, then back to GM."

The Damrons and the Williamsons didn't know each other back home — "Pike County will always be home to me," said Mabel, who lives in River Rouge. They met in Ilene's Restaurant in Ecorse in the early '70s.

"My wife and I were playing and singing at the restaurant," said George. "When we found out Mabel played, we all started playing together. The name of our group then is the same as it is now, the Kentucky String Band."

George's wife, Mary, died in 1978. "Every now and then Mabel and I will just get together and sit in the kitchen and play till we get tired," he said. "Ours is just traditional, old-time music. It was being played before they had guitars."

Mabel Damron and George Williamson, above in 1988, grew up with music. "My daddy played, my mother played and my grandpa played," says Damron. "My brother and my sister couldn't pick a lick. My daddy always told us to dance. He said if we dance a hole in the rug today, we'll get a new rug tomorrow." In Williamson's Kentucky home, "all our friends would get together for bean stringing or corn shucking or apple peeling, and music would be a part of the party." At right, the country music-making instruments, guitar, dulcimer, Autoharp, banjo and fiddle.

Susan Gosciniak and her mom, Dolores Di Curzio, shop at Eastern Market on a Saturday morning in 1990. Work goes on all day to prepare the family feast shown on Di Curzio's dining room table, below. "I love good food," says Susan, 28. "I was raised on it and I want to know how to prepare it myself. You can't get a homemade taste in a restaurant. It doesn't taste the same every time you make it; a pinch of basil may differ each time you cook. Good food is something you want to share. When I have a family, I want them to learn about the food. It's part of our culture. You have no identity if you don't know your heritage."

Dolores Di Curzio

cook

"My father was a fantastic cook," said Dolores Di Curzio.

"I remember him standing at the stove, making polenta, stirring it with a big wooden stick. He taught my mom how to cook, and then my mother taught me."

Di Curzio's father, Nazzareno, came to the United States in 1900 from Aquila in central Italy. "When you were a child in Italy back then, you had to learn how to cook when you learned how to walk," said Di Curzio, 57. "A meal wasn't just a bowl of cereal."

After roaming the United States for a few years, he came to Detroit and married a girl from Villa Latina, Italy. They opened a restaurant, named for her hometown, in a mainly Italian neighborhood behind Eastern Market.

"My father raised rabbits and pigeons, friends would bring him pheasants, and on Friday nights, he'd send me down to the fish market to buy a dollar's worth of oysters.

"As I was growing up, I learned to cook with dandelions and chicory because my father would cook with a lot of greens. And he taught me how to cook with beans. We made pasta and beans. Back then it was called a poor man's dish, but today, you go to a restaurant and it's very expensive," Di Curzio said.

"We didn't buy very many canned goods back then and still don't now," said Di Curzio, who lives in Mt. Clemens. "I was raised on Italian food, and I've raised my kids on it. I always made Italian food because my mother was always over at my house and I was afraid to make anything else."

Little Sonny Willis

blues player

Little Sonny Willis rehearses for a fund-raising concert for the Alger Theater on Detroit's east side in 1992. He has worked the nightclubs around Detroit and traveled the country to make recordings. When he came to Detroit in the 1950s and started in the business, he had to make his music sound like the big-name acts the people wanted to hear. But since the early 1990s, he has had his own recording company, and he's enjoying the chance to express himself. "I'm playing Little Sonny now," he says.

"One Christmas morning," said Aaron Willis, known as "Little Sonny" to blues fans around the country, "there was a plastic harmonica lying in the chair. My mother had bought me a 5-cent harmonica for Christmas.

"I was tickled to death and started trying to play it. From there on, I began to practice. I'd listen to all those different country-western singers and I'd listen to the harmonica players. Then I would practice to get the sounds I heard on the radio, and I started to fall in love with the black music I heard there."

Willis, 60, was born in Greensboro, Alabama, and moved to Detroit when he was 20 to live with his aunt. "I went from factory to factory trying to get a job and I couldn't find one, so I ended up working on a used car lot, cleaning up the automobiles."

In the evenings Willis would work the nightclubs, taking Polaroid pictures and selling them to the customers. "I would sit in with the band sometimes because I could sing and play the harmonica.

"One night, in 1955 at the Good Time Bar on Brush and Gratiot, I was sitting in for Washboard Willie, and the bar owner asked me, 'How would you like to work here with Washboard Willie?' and I asked, 'How much?'

"When I started out, I had to play Muddy Waters, Jimmy Reed, B.B. King, Lightnin' Hopkins, John Lee Hooker, Little Milton, Otis Rush," said Willis, who now plays and sings his own songs. "You had to play others before you got to know yourself. Now," he said, "I can play who I am."

Far left and above, Little Sonny performs at the Alger Theater benefit. Near left, backstage during a break in the show, Little Sonny talks with Louis Collins, a Detroit musician who goes by the name "Mr. Bo." Mr. Bo was playing with Washboard Willie in 1955 when Little Sonny was asked to play full-time at the Good Time Bar. "We go back to my beginning," says Little Sonny. After 35 years in the blues business, "I've prepared myself for this particular day, this time in my life, when I can present my music the best I can. I started singing when I was 7 years old. My mother would make me sing spiritual. She didn't want me to sing anything except spiritual songs, but I would sing the blues anyway."

Michigan Heritage Awards

Since 1985, Michigan State University Museum's Traditional Arts Program has given Michigan Heritage Awards annually to tradition bearers. With excellence and authenticity, these people sustain family or community folk life and dedicate themselves to passing it on. They bring honor to their communities, families and artistic forebears and are deserving of being called "masters."

Family members, neighbors and students of these master tradition bearers submit nominations each year to a review board in East Lansing. Winners are announced in the spring.

The Michigan Heritage Awards bring recognition to people who otherwise would go unnoticed except in their hometowns or among people who share their art. By singling out master tradition bearers, the Heritage Awards program makes it possible for the people of Michigan to know and appreciate the diversity of this state.

* Indicates Heritage Award winners whose stories are told in "Hands Across Michigan: Tradition Bearers."

Perry Allen
lumberjack, singer and teller of tall tales
award given posthumously

*Howard Armstrong
musician, p. 119

*Edward Baganz
Great Lakes captain, p. 124

*Amneh Baraka
embroiderer, p. 108

E.C. Beck
folk-life scholar
award given posthumously

*Edith Bondie
black ash basket maker, p. 48

Mattie Moss Clark
gospel singer, composer and director

Margarette Ernst
piano player

*Donna Esch
quilt maker, p. 55

Francis Jewell Gillespie
musician

Thelma James
folk-life educator

*Russell Johnson
lumberman's blacksmith, p. 2

Yvonne Walker Keshick
porcupine quill worker

*Dave Kober
fish decoy maker, p. 34

*Anna Lassila
rug maker, p. 18

Frank Mattison
fiddler

Lawrence (Honey) McCoy
piano player

Cecil McKenzie
piano player

*Art Moilanen
storytelling musician, p. 30

*Sonnie Perez
pinata maker, p. 116

*Les Raber
fiddler, p. 70

*Dan Rapelje
pigeon racer, p. 80

Agnes Rapp
black ash basket maker

*Doctor Ross
blues player, p. 100

*Sewing circle of St. Mary's Church in
Lake Leelanau
quilt makers, p. 57

*Harriet Shedawin
black ash basket maker, p. 11

*Jay Stephan
Au Sable boat builder, p. 40

*Don Stevens
tribal elder, p. 95

*Bud Stewart
lure maker, p. 44

*Eli Thomas
tribal elder, p. 94

*Jingo Viitala Vachon
storytelling musician, p. 31

Sippie Wallace
blues singer

Ivan Walton
Great Lakes folklore educator
award given posthumously

*Julia Wesaw
black ash basket maker, p. 93

*Edmund Whitepigeon
black ash basket maker, p. 92

*Jim Wicks
duck decoy carver, p. 22

*Little Sonny Willis
blues player, p. 132

Suggested readings

Beck, E.C. "Lore of the Lumber Camps." University of Michigan Press, 1948.

Castle, Beatrice Hansom. "The Grand Island Story." The John M. Longyear Research Library (Marquette), 1987.

Catton, Bruce. "Waiting for the Morning Train: An American Boyhood." Wayne State University Press, 1972 and 1987.

Clifton, James; Cornell, George; and McClurken, James. "People of the Three Fires: The Ottawa, Potawatomi and Ojibwa of Michigan." Grand Rapids Inter-Tribal Council, 1986.

Dewhurst, C. Kurt; and Lockwood, Yvonne R., eds. "Michigan Folklife Reader." Michigan State University Press, 1988.

Dewhurst, C. Kurt; and MacDowell, Marsha. "Rainbows in the Sky: The Folk Art of Michigan in the Twentieth Century." Michigan State University Museum, 1978.

Dobson, Pamela J., ed. "The Tree That Never Dies: Oral History of the Michigan Indians." Grand Rapids Public Library, 1978.

Dorson, Richard M. "Bloodstoppers and Bearwalkers: Folk Traditions of the Upper Peninsula" (1956); "Negro Folktales in Michigan" (1956). Harvard University Press.

Donnelly, Joseph P. "Jacques Marquette, S.J., 1637-1675." Loyola Press, 1968.

Eberly, Carol, ed. "Our Michigan: Ethnic Tales and Recipes." Eberly Press (East Lansing), 1979.

Fasquelle, Ethel Rowan. "When Michigan was Young." Avery Color Studios (Marquette), 1981.

"Festival of Michigan Folklife Program Book." Michigan State University Museum, annually from 1987.

Gardner, Emelyn Elizabeth; and Chickering, Geraldine Jencks, eds. "Ballads and Songs of Southern Michigan." Folklore Associates (Hatboro, Pa.), 1939 and 1967.

Gage, Cully. "The Northwoods Reader" (1977); "Tales of the Old U.P." (1981); "What? Another Northwoods Reader" (1987); "A Love Affair with the U.P." (1988). Avery Color Studios.

Grimm, Joe, ed. "Michigan Voices: Our State's History in the Words of the People Who Lived It." Detroit Free Press and Wayne State University Press, 1987.

Hathaway, Richard, ed. "Michigan: Visions of Our Past." Michigan State University Press, 1987.

Hobart, Henry. "Copper Country Journal: The Diary of Schoolmaster Henry Hobart, 1863-1864." Philip P. Mason, ed. Wayne State University Press, 1991.

Johnston, Basil. "Ojibway Heritage." University of Nebraska Press, 1976.

Kenneway, Eric. "Complete Origami." St. Martin's Press, 1987.

Kinietz, W. Vernon. "The Indians of the Western Great Lakes, 1615-1760." University of Michigan Press, 1965.

Kohl, J.G. "Kitchi-Gamu: Wanderings 'Round Lake Superior." Rose & Haines (Minneapolis), 1956.

Lockwood, Yvonne R.; Dewhurst, C. Kurt; and MacDowell, Marsha. "Michigan: Whose Story? A Celebration of the State's Traditions." Michigan State University Museum, 1985.

MacDowell, Marsha; and Fitzgerald, Ruth D., eds. "Michigan Quilts: 150 Years of a Textile Tradition." Michigan State University Museum, 1987.

Martin, John Bartlow. "Call It North Country: The Story of Upper Michigan." Wayne State University Press, 1944 and 1986.

Massie, Larry B. "Copper Trails and Iron Rails" (1989); "Voyages into Michigan's Past" (1988). Avery Color Studios. "Pig Boats and River Hogs" (1990); "Potawatomi Tears and Petticoat Pioneers" (1992). The Priscilla Press (Allegan Forest).

Massie, Larry B. and Massie, Priscilla. "Walnut Pickles and Watermelon Cake: A Century of Michigan Cooking." Wayne State University Press, 1990.

Love, Edmund G. "The Situation in Flushing." Wayne State University Press, 1965 and 1987.

Lutes, Della T. "The Country Kitchen." Wayne State University Press, 1936 and 1992.

McClurken James M. "Gah-Baeh-Jhagwah-Buk/The Way It Happened: A Visual History of the Little Traverse Bay Band of Odawa." Michigan State University Museum, 1991.

The Joanna Circle of Sion Lutheran Church, Chatham, eds. "Northcountry Kitchens Cookbook." Avery Color Studios, 1980.

Peck, John M.; and Sparks, Jared. "Makers of American History: Daniel Bocrt, Robert Cavelier De La Salle, and Father Marquette." J.A. Hill (New York), 1904.

Perkins, Stan. "Lore of the Wolverine Country." Broadblade Press (Swartz Creek), 1984.

Romig, Walter. "Michigan Place Names." Wayne State University Press, 1986 reprint from 1973.

Rydholm, C. Fred. "Superior Heartland: A Backwoods History." Vol. 1, Books I and II; Vol. 2, Books III and IV. Published by the author in Marquette, 1989.

"The Old Settlers: A Nation Within Itself." Old Settlers' Reunion Association (Remus).

Schoolcraft, Henry Rowe. "The Hiawatha Legends: The Myth of Hiawatha and Other Oral Legends, Mythologic and Allegoric, of the North American Indians" (1984 reprint from 1856). Avery Color Studios. "Schoolcraft's Indian Legends." Mentor L. Williams and Philip P. Mason, eds. (1962 and 1991, drawn from Schoolcraft's "Algic Researches," 1839). Michigan State University Press.

Voelker, John (Robert Traver). "Trout Madness" (1984 reprint from 1960). Peregrine Smith Books (Salt Lake City). "Laughing Whitefish" (1983). McGraw-Hill.

Williams, Elizabeth Whitney. "A Child of the Sea and Life Among the Mormons on Beaver Island." Beaver Island Historical Society (1983 reprint from 1905).

Wilson, Ben. "The Amazing Curative Powers of Black Home Remedies and Other Elements of Folk Wisdom in Rural Southwestern Michigan." Negro History Bulletin, 1982.

Woodford, Frank B. "Lewis Cass: The Last Jeffersonian." Rutgers University Press, 1950.

Other sources:
◆ Great Lakes Books, Wayne State University Press
◆ Michigan State University Museum
◆ Michigan State University Press
◆ Bureau of History, Michigan Department of State
◆ Michigan History Magazine
◆ Michigan Natural Resources Magazine

Author's notes

Cameras: All the photographs in "Hands Across Michigan: Tradition Bearers" were made using Nikon FM2 and F4, 35mm cameras with the following Nikkor Lenses:

24mm f/2
35mm f/2
60mm f/2.8 macro
85mm f/2
105mm f/2.5
135mm f/2
180mm f/2.8
300mm f/4

Film: The color photographs were shot on Kodak Extar 25 and Kodak Gold Plus/Ektapress color negative film, ASA 100 to 1600. The black-and-white photographs on pages 34, 35, 36, 37, 42, 43, 44, 45, 46, 47, 48, 66, 72, 92, 93, 98, 99, 100, 101, 102, 103, 104, 105, 106, 110, 111, 112, 113, 114, 115, 116, 117, 137, 138, 139, 140, 143, 144, 145, 146, 147, 149, 150 and 151 were made from color negative film. The rest were printed from Kodak T-max 400 ASA film, rated from 200 to 1600 ASA.

Text: For words with varying spellings, Michigan State University Museum was the authority on Indian terms and Merriam-Webster's Collegiate Dictionary, Tenth Edition, on other terms whenever it was appropriate to use a generally accepted spelling.

Many of the stories in this book are based on articles written by Alan R. Kamuda and published in the Detroit Free Press from 1987 to 1993. All have been updated to reflect current ages and activities of the subjects.

Index of tradition bearers

Megwech

In the language of the Ojibwa, Ottawa and Potawatomi, it's *megwech;* in Swedish, *tack;* in Finnish, *kiitos.* In German, it's the familiar *danke schoen.* In Chinese, it's *hsieh hsieh; shoukran* in Arabic; *dziekuje* in Polish; *dhanyavad* in Hindi; *gracias* in Spanish; *danku* in Flemish; *arigato* in Japanese; *fala* in Macedonian; *grazie* in Italian. In English, it's thank you.

At Michigan State University Museum, thank you to Drs. C. Kurt Dewhurst, Marsha MacDowell and Yvonne Lockwood for greeting my ideas with enthusiasm.

Thank you to Dr. Laurie Kay Sommers and Lynne Swanson for working with me and wanting to expand the photographic collection. Thank you, Terry Hanson, for listening to my problems; and thank you, Chantel Cummings, for taking care of them and for handling all the negatives with the utmost care — and for laughing at my jokes.

Thank you, Thomas L. Jones, executive director of the Historical Society of Michigan, for guiding me through the publishing maze. I hope it is a walk we can make again soon.

And thank you to the Detroit Free Press:

To publisher Neal Shine for your faith in my work, Dave Robinson for your interest in the quality of this project, Mike Smith for allowing me to report the stories I find important, Marcia Prouse for teaching me, Diane Bond for making most of the prints in "Hands," and Tony Spina for taking my photograph for the jacket. Thank you, Martha Thierry, for the maps of Michigan and thank you, Pat Foley, for dotting all the i's.

And to Lee Yarosh and Nancy Dunn, *megwech.* Thank you for becoming part of "Hands Across Michigan." It could not have been done without you. Thank you, Lee, for the design and the layout; and thank you, Nancy, for making it look as if I know the English language. You both have made this book a work of art.

To the people who are the tradition bearers of "Hands Across Michigan," thank you. Thank you for allowing me into your lives. I hope that there is at least one person who comes to each of you to learn your art so that it can be passed on to the children.